W9-ATY-506

Mommy
Grace

Mommy Grace

Erasing Your Mommy Guilt

Dr. Sheila Schuller Coleman

NEW YORK   BOSTON   NASHVILLE

Copyright © 2009 by Sheila Schuller Coleman

All rights reserved. Except as permitted under the U.S. Copyright Act of 1976, no part of this publication may be reproduced, distributed, or transmitted in any form or by any means, or stored in a database or retrieval system, without the prior written permission of the publisher.

Unless otherwise noted, Scripture quotations are from the Holy Bible, New International Version®. Copyright © 1973, 1978, 1984 by International Bible Society. Used by permission of Zondervan Publishing House. All rights reserved.

Scripture quotations noted NASB are from the New American Standard Bible®. Copyright © 1960, 1962, 1963, 1968, 1971, 1972, 1973, 1975, 1977, 1995 by The Lockman Foundation. Used by permission.

Scripture quotations noted NKJV are from the New King James Version, copyright © 1982 by Thomas Nelson, Inc. Used by permission. All rights reserved.

FaithWords

Hachette Book Group

237 Park Avenue

New York, NY 10017

Visit our Web site at www.faithwords.com.

Book design by Fearn Cutler de Vicq

Printed in the United States of America

First Edition: April 2009

10   9   8   7   6   5   4   3   2   1

FaithWords is a division of Hachette Book Group, Inc.

The FaithWords name and logo are trademarks of Hachette Book Group, Inc.

Library of Congress Cataloging-in-Publication Data

Coleman, Sheila Schuller.

Mommy grace : erasing your mommy guilt / Sheila Schuller Coleman. — 1st ed.

p. cm.

ISBN: 978-0-446-54541-9

1. Mothers—Religious life.   2. Motherhood—Religious aspects—Christianity.

I. Title.

BV4529.18.C64 2009

248.8'431—dc22

2008022338

This book is dedicated to all of the mommies
who have graced me with their presence —
as friends, colleagues, and family.

Contents

Acknowledgments

I am indebted to the tireless support and loving encouragement of my beloved husband, Jim. I am a writer today because he persistently believed in me and nudged me to give it a try.

This book absolutely would not have been possible without my four precious sons, who provided most of the material, not to mention the tons of mommy guilt! They brought more joy to my life than I could ever imagine. My buttons burst with love and pride whenever I am with them or even think of them!

I am eternally grateful for the support of my patient, understanding mother, who helped me get up time after time when I was knocked down by mommy guilt. I am grateful for both my parents, who challenged me to always keep my words positive, whether they were written or spoken.

I also need to acknowledge the support and encouragement of my baby sister, Gretchen, an awesome mother who never tires of reminding me, as an author or as a mother, of the grace of Jesus. Her influence underscores many of the lessons found in this book.

This book would not have been possible without my faithful assistant and friend, Myra Hammond, who opened my eyes to mommy guilt. As both of us struggled to raise sons the same ages, while working in a school where, ironically, we were the last ones to know what was happening, Myra was the first to help me see that I wasn't the only one suffering from mommy guilt.

Also, I am indebted to Carole Barber, Linda Lind, Kristen Mulady, and Kristi Thomas — moms, all — not to mention a school principal and school secretaries who are there every morning to help countless mommies and children throughout the school day. Even so, they always had time, between phone calls, bloody noses, and vomiting children, to listen or read and give me honest feedback.

Last but not least, this would not have been possible without wise guidance and counsel from Sealy Yates and Jeana Ledbetter. It was their patient prodding that helped clarify the focus and format of this book.

Holly Halverson, an amazing editor, tied all of the corners together into one neat package and made sure that I covered all my bases without being misunderstood, before this went into "unforgivable print."

This book was a joy to work on from beginning to end. That is due, in large part, to the fact that this project was a team effort and, most important, an excuse to spend time with all of you. As a result, you brought a deeper awareness of grace to my life and others. For that I am most grateful! Thank you — all of you!

Introduction

*A*s the mother of four sons, all born within a span of seven years (Jason, Christopher, Scott, and Nicholas), I have often said that I never appreciated the cross of Christ more than when I became a mother. While I had envisioned and anticipated the advent of my children with unrealistic and romantic notions that mothering would be easy, I found to my great shock that it was the most difficult task I had ever undertaken. I not only was filled with apprehension, I also lived many days under the cloud of guilt and fear that I was not measuring up to what I thought I should be as a good mother.

As the principal of a private Christian school, I have since worked with many other young mothers and learned that I am not alone in my feelings of inadequacy. Indeed, mommy guilt appears to be a struggle that plagues nearly all of us mothers on a regular basis.

Every morning I see the moms who had bad starts to their day because they end up in the school office getting a tardy slip. I hear about the morning from you-know-where as they inevitably mutter something under their breath that tells me they feel like bad moms. Their source of guilt can be anything from sleeping through the alarm to not helping their children with a spelling test or not making an organic spread for their children's lunch. But mommy guilt really ramps up when I have to call them because their child has made a poor choice at school — anywhere from pushing in line to urinating in the sink (kindergarten!).

Whenever I talk to young mothers who are beating themselves up with mommy guilt, I say, "This is a school where you will be loved and forgiven."

I wish I'd had someone to reassure me of this when I was a young mother. I wish I had realized that what I was going through was universal. Unfortunately I was too proud to admit my feelings to anyone. I thought if I pretended to have my act together, others would continue to love and respect me. I was afraid that if other mothers found out what an "impostor" I was, they would look down on me.

The truth was there were many times I lost my temper with my children and yelled at them, especially in the morning in my quest to get them to school on time. There were times I was too tired to read to them or play with them. I frequently found that I was neglecting my daily quiet time with the Lord because I just didn't have the energy or the desire. Besides, I had asked Him to help me be a better mother, and it didn't seem as though He was answering my prayers. At the time of my deepest need, I felt the farthest from Him. All of this (and much, much more) added up to a mountain of mommy guilt.

Mommy guilt for me was at its worst when, as a working mom, I woke up to one of my sons throwing up or running a fever. Of course, it always seemed to happen on the day when I had a major presentation to make, or a meeting with someone who had flown in from out of town, or just after I'd used my last sick day. Those situations were always a no-win, and I was never fun to be around on those days.

Mommy guilt escalated when the boys got into their teens. What if they didn't turn out well? It would be my fault! I imagined them lying on psychologists' couches, replaying all my shortcomings as a mother. It didn't help that I was an educator and an administrator. What if they did something that would embarrass me? What credibility could I have as an "expert" if my own sons were not all I thought they should be?

Today—now that my sons are grown, doing well, and they love me anyway—I can release a deep sigh of relief. I now look back and shake my head at how foolish I was. I did a lot of things right as a young mother. I also made more than my share of mistakes. In the final analysis, the biggest mistake I made was worrying too much, berating myself too much, and subsequently losing out on much of the joy of being a mother.

Yet, if I hadn't been a mother of four sons, I think I would have always taken the cross of Jesus Christ for granted. I wasn't one of those girls who rebelled as a youth, so admittedly, as a young woman I felt quite smug and superior, spiritually speaking. But once I became a mother I threw myself at the foot of the cross daily. As a result I experienced the beauty, the wonder, the overwhelming gratitude that come from knowing I have been redeemed and forgiven, and I am loved just as I am. That is perhaps the greatest gift I received as a young mother!

My hope and prayer for you is that through this book you will learn you are not alone. Most of all, I pray you will realize that mommy guilt is actually a gift—an opportunity—to experience mommy grace. In the process, your love affair with Christ will be magnified and you will never be the same. If mommy guilt teaches you that, if mommy guilt pushes you to the foot of the cross, then you will see — it is indeed a gift. Mommy grace is yours for the taking. Do not delay. Reach out and take it — now!

Mommy Grace

Response-Ability

*M*y newborn son lay sleeping in my arms. The over-whelming responsibility of this new little life weighed heavily on me. What if I failed to be all that he needed in a mother? Would his *emotional* well-being suffer if I gave him too much attention? Too little attention? Would his *physical* health suffer if I didn't nurse him long enough? Or if I ate the wrong foods? Would his *spirituality* suffer if I didn't have the answers to his questions? Would I mess up his whole life just by not being a good enough mother?

I felt powerless to be all that my baby needed me to be. How could I possibly measure up?

All the dreams of being a new mother, the thrill I had felt while preparing his nursery, were now dispelled as the reality of the immense responsibilities of a baby hit me full force. Struggling to overcome my fears, I nuzzled his tawny, fuzzy head. "Help me, Lord," I prayed. "I don't know what I'm doing. I can't do this. I love him so much! I am so afraid of messing up. I need Your help!"

Then, because He knew I was desperate, the Lord gave me this thought: *"You're making it too complicated. It's actually very simple.*

Your sole responsibility is—response-ability. Just respond *to Jason's needs to the best of your* ability *and leave the results to Me."*

Wow! What a weight fell from my shoulders that day. What a gift from God!

All the how-to books and magazine articles I had read with their advice were messing with my mind. One word from God swept this all away. One godly how-to took the place of the myriad shoulds.

Two-step mothering. Now, that I could handle!

1) Responding—that was much more doable than controlling.
2) Leaving the results to God—that was much more desirable than being the final answer.

Was this the last time I felt overwhelmed by my responsibilities as a mother? I wish! Like every other mother I have ever talked with, I have questioned my abilities as a mother nearly every day. I continue to worry that I am messing up.

But whenever I take the time to remember my word of encouragement from God, I once again feel peace and regain clarity in how God wants me to do this awesome task: just *respond* to my children's needs to the best of my *ability* and leave the results to Him!

Responsibility is response-ability—
And leaving the results to God!

My grace is sufficient for you,
for my power is made perfect in weakness.

— 2 CORINTHIANS 12:9

Lord,
Thank You for the gift of children —
    And what they teach us about You
    And how much You love us!

This love we feel for our children,
    Although it consumes us,
        Almost smothering us in its intensity
    Although it triggers in us
    An irrational need to
        Protect at all costs and
        Provide whatever they need

This love we feel for our children
    Is but a slivered reflection
    Of what You feel for us
        Your precious children
You, who did not spare Your own Son,
    Will surely provide everything we need.

Thank You, Lord, for understanding
        Our love
        Our fears

Help us *today* to just
        Respond to their needs
        To the best of our ability
        and leave the results to You.

                Amen.

Fallen—but Forgiven

*D*irty mixing bowls were piled high in the sink. Flour dusted the counters and even the floor. I had once again allowed myself to become overambitious and was attempting to make too many complicated dishes for Christmas Eve. Whom was I trying to impress? My husband's family, of course! And Jason, six months old, was not cooperating. He wanted my attention, but I didn't have time to play with him. The family was coming over to our house for a candlelight buffet right after Christmas Eve services, and I was running a day late as usual.

Jason scooted around the kitchen in his walker, getting underfoot. Because I was running late, my patience was beginning to wear thin. Balancing too many bowls, spoons, pots, and pans with a baby on wheels that I kept tripping over was just not working. But, since it was a balmy, sunny California winter day, I thought maybe he'd be happier out on the patio (or so I rationalized). And I certainly would be able to juggle better without having to dodge hot wheels.

I picked Jason up in his walker, set him down outside on the patio, and ran back into the kitchen, just a few steps away. I felt sure he would be safe, as I could see him through the sliding glass door while I worked. Great idea, I thought!

But I had no sooner returned to the kitchen and had just begun to knead the Christmas bread when I heard a piercing cry. To my horror, I saw my baby lying facedown, feet kicking in the air. His wheels had snagged at the end of the patio and his walker had upended, hurtling his little face into the rocky soil that bordered our patio.

My heart racing, I ran over, gathered him in my arms, and saw to my utter dismay bloody scratches on his dirt-smeared face. With a soft, warm washcloth I managed to wipe his face off even as he cried in pain. I held him close, rocking him, cradling him, until he cried himself to sleep. The bake-off in the kitchen no longer seemed important. I had hurt my baby—all because I had wanted to impress others!

I felt like the worst mother in the world. Guilt began to wrap its ugly, suffocating tentacles around my soul: I should have had more sense. I should have been more patient. I should have been more careful. Instead, I had been negligent and my baby had been hurt in the process. Even though I was relieved that he hadn't been hurt worse, I still felt terrible.

How could I go to Christmas Eve service and show my face? I had no business going to church. Some Christian mother I was! I couldn't let on to anyone that I had failed my baby so miserably. Somehow, I managed to put on my best fake smile and go to the service. But as I sat next to my husband, Jim, that night, I thought, *It's a good thing they don't know what a bad mother I am!*

The tentacles of guilt by now had a death grip on me. Even the inspiring music couldn't ease their clasp on my soul. Even the Scriptures were unable to bring release. I felt as if I would suffocate. In desperation, I pleaded, "Lord, forgive me!"

Never was there a more penitent sinner. Then, in answer to my plea, I once again replayed Jason's accident in my mind's eye, as I had over and over again all day. I could see him running with his little legs as fast as he could go toward the end of the patio, his wheels catching on the edge of the patio and suddenly catapulting through the air. But in my mental replay, this time as he was falling, facedown into the rocky soil, I suddenly saw something new: two large, gentle hands swept into the picture, cushioning his fall. This time I saw my baby falling into the gracious hands of God.

This new, revised vision from God caused the shackles of my guilt to spring open. I was freed! Liberated! The grace of God that was His Christmas gift to me enveloped me like a warm, comforting blanket. Because Jesus had been born, I was forgiven. Because God was there to catch my son when I had let him down, I could forgive myself and trust that God would be my rear guard, cleaning up my messes. Because Jesus had been born, I could put my son in the hands of God and the pierced hands of His Son, my Lord and Savior. What a promise! What a hope! Grace was born once again in the heart of this young mother. Hallelujah!

God is there to catch us when we fall . . .
To pick us up when we stumble . . .
To clean up our messes!
What a priceless gift!

All have sinned and fall short of the glory of God,
and are justified freely by his grace
through the redemption that came by Christ Jesus.

—ROMANS 3:23–24

Jesus,
I let my child down today. . . .
I let him fall and get hurt . . .
I wasn't there for him when he needed me.

Thank You for holding out Your hands
Pierced hands . . .
      To catch my child . . .
      To catch me . . .
      To forgive me
And give me the grace to forgive myself!
Let Your grace be born in me today.

Amen.

The "Shoulds" and "Should Nots" Are Driving Me to My Knees!

- ❧ I should have spent more time playing with my children.
- ❧ I should not have yelled at them so much.
- ❧ I should have made more healthy food for my sons.
- ❧ I should not have let them eat so much candy.
- ❧ I should have done more physical activities with my children.
- ❧ I should not have allowed them to watch so much TV.
- ❧ I should have spent more time praying for my children.
- ❧ I should have trusted more.
- ❧ I should not have given in to my fears.

Writing this list was a piece of cake. Truth be told, I had to force myself to stop or it could have gone on for the rest of this book. I hear from moms all the time about how their "shoulds" and "should nots" eat at their happiness and contribute to their mounting mommy guilt. Mommy guilt is exacerbated by the fact that we moms are inundated with contradictory articles and books and advice from well-meaning friends. In the process, we become confused and overwhelmed and feel as if we are completely botching the very thing that means the most to us! As a result, we moms are in a no-win, mommy-guilt-ridden situation.

When Jason was just an infant, I took him to the park one day. He was lying on a blanket under a tree while I read a book. Another young mommy came and sat by us. She introduced herself. I thought, *Wonderful, a new friend.*

She looked at my book and asked, "What are you reading?"

I showed her the cover of some book on how to build your infant's self-esteem.

"Oh," she said with a sneer, "you're one of those mothers who read!" Then she got up, took her baby and left. I never saw her again.

"What's wrong with reading?" I asked the woman who by now was out of sight.

Of course, it didn't take long to see how frustrating how-to mommy books could be. In fact, I can't say that many, if any, of them really helped. All they seemed to do was confuse me or frustrate me and add to my lists of "shoulds" and "should nots," which in turn added to my growing mountain of mommy guilt.

I'm afraid that I eventually became one of those mothers who didn't read anymore — at least not self-help mommy books. So, what am I doing writing this book? Good question! Well, I have intentionally not written a how-to book. *Mommy Grace* is merely a book to encourage mommies, because that's what we need the most. We already know how to do it. Intuitively we already know what we *should* and *should not* do. We don't need to add to our already overwhelming list.

Nevertheless, as a young mommy, even though I was well aware of the psychological principle that I should not succumb to "shoulds" and "should nots," I couldn't seem to help myself. Even today, the more I think about avoiding these little guilt traps, the more likely I am to get snared in them.

Paul described this condition aptly in Romans: "I do not understand what I do. For what I want to do I do not do, but what I hate I do.... What a wretched [mom] I am! Who will rescue me from this body of death? Thanks be to God—through Jesus Christ our Lord!" (Rom. 7:15, 24–25).

Perhaps the secret to being free from the litany of "shoulds" and "should nots" is to realize and accept the fact that we can't do it. Only God can. We can be liberated only by the grace of Jesus Christ! This unbearable, wretched condition can hold us captive—unless we turn our lives over to Jesus and accept His grace. We need to fall helpless to our knees and openly admit, "I can't do this! I need Your help, Lord! Save me from the tyranny of 'shoulds' and 'should nots'!" Then the guilt becomes a gift—propelling us to our knees and into our Savior's arms, where we can find mommy grace—and freedom.

*I should accept the grace of Christ
That frees me from mommy guilt!*

What, then, shall we say in response to this?
If God is for us, who can be against us?
He who did not spare his own Son, but gave him up
for us all —
how will he not also, along with him,
graciously give us all things?

—Romans 8:31–32

Heavenly Father,
As I come to the end of the day
There are so many things I would have
     Done differently or
     Not done at all.

I should have listened to my kids more
I should have hugged my kids more
I should have played and laughed with my kids

I should not have yelled at my kids
I should not have pushed aside their tugs
I should not have tuned out their cries

I should have spent more time talking to You
I should have taken the time to read Your love letter to me

Give me the grace to forgive myself
And the courage to try my best tomorrow
Even knowing that I might fail to keep my priorities
In their place,
My focus on my kids and You.

Amen.

In Better Hands Than Mine

*W*eighing in at a robust ten pounds, four ounces at birth, Christopher was the picture of a big, healthy baby. He was a content and happy baby. I couldn't wait for his three-month checkup with the pediatrician to hear how well he was doing. But when I undressed him and laid him on the examining table, the doctor's brow furrowed.

"How long has he been doing this?"

"Doing what?"

"Pulling in like this every time he breathes."

She pointed out how Christopher's chest caved in every time he took a breath.

"I don't know. I've never noticed. Is there something wrong?"

"This isn't normal. In fact, I want you to take him directly over to a specialist. I will call ahead and make sure he gets seen immediately."

Her words and tone made me nervous, but she was only sending me to a specialist. If it were really serious, she'd be sending me to the hospital, right?

The doctor she sent me to was an allergist. He saw Christopher within minutes of my arriving at his office. He too seemed very concerned about the pulling in Christopher's chest.

"I'm going to give him a shot of epinephrine. I want you to wait here for a half hour. We will see how he does. If it gets better, you can take him home, but if not, you will have to take him to the hospital."

The gravity of the situation was making me more and more nervous. But every time I looked at Chris, he appeared so content and healthy. Surely this couldn't be anything to worry too much about. Sure enough, when the doctor checked on him later, he said, "Good. He's breathing much better." He sent me home with instructions and a return appointment.

However, that Friday night right after dinner the doctor called me at home. "Sheila, I am getting ready to go into a concert and will be turning my pager off. Before I do I want you to go check Christopher's chest for me. Is he pulling when he breathes? I also want a respiratory count."

Man, these doctors sure are thorough, I thought as I checked on my baby. I was impressed with the care the doctors were providing, but at the same time it made me wonder if I needed to be more worried than I was.

I reported the respiratory count to the doctor and he said, "Sounds good. But if he begins to run a temperature or his breathing gets more rapid or labored, call me immediately!"

This inordinate amount of personal concern from a doctor got my attention. I checked on Christopher frequently throughout the night and the next morning. Then, around noon, I realized something was terribly wrong. Christopher shivered, or shook—was it a seizure? I couldn't tell, but he was hot to the touch, and when I took his temperature it was 104 degrees. My baby—my healthy, robust Christopher—appeared to be in real danger. *Are you going to be okay?* I wondered as I called the doctor.

"Get Chris to the emergency room immediately. I will call ahead and tell them you are coming. I want them to do a spinal tap."

A spinal tap? I knew what that meant. They were concerned he might have spinal meningitis. My voice choked as I told Jim what the doctor had said. By now as we raced our baby to the emergency room, Christopher was really fussy and hot. There was nothing I could do to console him.

When the nurse in the hospital took him from me, she said, "You wait here. It's a painful procedure. It's best you not be there to see it."

When the door closed behind her, I looked frantically for some privacy. I knew I couldn't hold it back much longer. I locked myself in the nearest bathroom and bent over double and allowed the silent wails to pour out of me as I heard my baby's piercing cries of pain coming from down the hall.

When I returned the nurse told me, "It's positive. He has spinal meningitis. We are preparing a room for him in the intensive care unit." She put hot, fussy Christopher—dressed only in a diaper to help bring his temperature down—back in my arms. I followed the nurse as she led the way through the hospital corridors and through the ominous stainless-steel doors marked "Pediatric Intensive Care Unit."

Watching the team hook my baby up to the monitors, hearing him crying inconsolably, it all seemed surreal. *How can this be?* I thought. "Can't you give him anything for the pain?"

"No. The infection is in the fluid surrounding his brain and his spine. Consequently, any medication affecting the nervous system can have adverse effects and he could end up being in more pain. We will attempt to bring down the fever through external temperature controls."

I stood by Christopher's cold crib, tall metal bars barricading my baby from me. By then he was hoarse from crying and had wires coming from him everywhere. I asked, "Can I hold him?"

"It will hurt him more if you do. Spinal meningitis causes the neck to stiffen, and he is in less pain lying on the firm bed than he would be if you held him."

All I could do was stand there helplessly and watch my baby suffer.

His doctor said to me, "Sheila, go home. I see mothers stay and when their babies are better they go home to worn out moms. Christopher will need a rested mother when we send him home in a week."

I took her advice because I trusted her and because it hurt too much to watch him, unable to do anything. But when I got home I walked down to his nursery, leaned over his empty crib where Jim had placed a tiny baby-blue Bible on his pillow, and cried and cried.

The doctor meant well, but I couldn't sleep. All night long I tossed and turned and thought of the empty crib at the end of the hall. My arms ached to hold my round bundle of joy. Finally, around four a.m., I couldn't take it any longer. I went downstairs and sat in the big, soft chair where I usually sat to nurse Chris. It faced the fireplace where Jim and I had hung a picture of Christ. I looked at the picture and prayed, "Lord, I have never needed You more. If ever I needed You to be real to me—this is the time!"

I closed my eyes, and in my mind I could see Jesus. I couldn't see His face clearly, but I could see—actually I could also feel—Him cradling Christopher in His arms. Then I heard

Him say to me, *"You are very proud of him, Sheila. But in the final analysis he is not your child. He is Mine."*

Now, most young mothers will tell you that they have to resist the urge to take their babies back from others who are holding them, because maternal instinct tells you your baby is really comfortable only in your arms. But when I saw Jesus holding Christopher, I had no urge to take him. I could feel that he was just as at home in Christ's arms as he was in mine. It was that feeling — the reassurance that Christopher was not just in good hands, he was in God's hands — that enabled me to give him completely over to God. It was then and there that Jesus gave me the peace that passes understanding and carried me through the next week in the hospital and through the physical therapy for the months that followed. (We needed to alleviate the tight muscles that were, in his case, a residual effect of the meningitis that could adversely impact his development.)

It was in that moment I learned to let go of the need to be in control and learned that God was my true source of power. Trusting in *Him* rather than myself — that was the secret, and that was the lesson I learned through this. But I was enabled to hand over my baby to Him only because the hands into which I relinquished him were loving, strong, and powerful.

Out of my hands — and into His Hands
Loving Hands
Pierced Hands
Powerful Hands!

I trust in you, O LORD;
I say, "You are my God."
My times are in your hands.

—PSALM 31:14–15

Lord,
These precious children
They do not belong to me
They are Your creation
        You made them
        You gave them
To me to love and enjoy for today

So, I give them back to You
I place them in the best hands possible . . .
        Loving hands . . .
        Pierced hands . . .
        Powerful hands.

Out of my hands —
        And into better hands
        Your hands!

                Amen.

Turning Over the Keys of My Life

I had thought I was the queen of locking my keys in my car. In fact, my husband had grown tired of my calling him from a pay phone (this was before cell phones) to drive thirty miles one way from work to bail out the boys and me. He finally drilled a hole through a spare key and screwed it behind the license plate. "That way, all you have to do is borrow a kitchen knife [my favorite tool!], and you can get back into the car!" I blush to admit how many times I had to go into a small diner and borrow a table knife.

Sue was one of the few friends with whom I felt I could be completely honest. I could confess all my inadequacies to her. Our children were the same ages. She had three to my four. Both of us had careers. When I told her one day about Jim's solution to my problem with keys, she laughed and said, "Oh, Sheila! That's nothing! Do you know what I did one day?"

And so she told me the following story:

It was raining cats and dogs. I had all three of the kids with me. We were rushing from one store to another and we were all hungry. When I saw a McDonald's I pulled over. As you know, balancing the kids is hard enough without rain, but with the rain, I was also trying to keep all of us dry — which was virtually impossible!

It was a relief to get into the dry shelter of McDonald's and to just sit for a few minutes. After we had finished eating, however, I went to get my keys but I couldn't find them anywhere. Suddenly I realized that I must have thrown them away with all the trash. I went to the store manager, explained my situation, and they began to tear through all the grimy, yucky trash cans, looking for my keys.

But they couldn't find them. I began to wonder if I had locked them in the car. So I helped the kids get back into their rain gear, gathered everything up, and we sloshed through the puddles and the rain back to the car.

Much to my surprise, there to my horror, the car door was open! Rain was pouring in. Not only that, the keys were in the ignition, and the car was still running!

"The car was still running? The door was open!? Sue, your car could have been stolen!"

"You're telling me!"

Sue and I were dangerous, I was learning, when it came to keys!

Driving in the rain with children can be a metaphor for mothering these days. It can be harrowing, dangerous, and challenging to navigate the potholes in the midst of too many distractions. Even though we may feel overwhelmed and inadequate when we find ourselves at the wheel of a car full of kids, driving in the rains of life, it is important to commend ourselves. Why? Because we had the courage to get in the car, turn on the ignition, step on the gas, and say "Yes" to an awesome call. After all, God can't do anything with us if we are still in park and the steering wheel is locked. We have taken the most courageous step. We said yes to God's dream for our lives.

It is important for us to know that what we are doing as mothers is an awesome, and at times impossible, task. It is not a call we can manage all by ourselves. It is a dream so big that we must have God's guidance if we are going to succeed! The good news is — we don't have to be the drivers. We can turn over the keys of our lives, we can count on God to navigate us through the dangerous intersections, to come alongside and redirect us when we are going the wrong way, and to even redeem us when we crash and burn.

You had the courage to say yes to the dream, now have the courage to turn over the keys and let Him drive the dream. Trust that God will not let you — or His dream for you — down. He will never mislead you.

Get up and go
Trust God to guide
Then sit back
And enjoy the ride!

✦

Since you are my rock and my fortress,
for the sake of your name lead and guide me.

—Psalm 31:3

I will lead the blind by ways they have not known,
along unfamiliar paths I will guide them;
I will turn the darkness into light before them
and make the rough places smooth.
These are the things I will do;
I will not forsake them.

—Isaiah 42:16

✦

Dear gracious, guiding God,
Thank You that I do not have to do this alone!
I did my part to get in the car
To turn on the ignition
To get out of park
In so doing I . . .
Took steps in faith
Trusting that You will now take the wheel
And guide me in the right direction

Help me turn over the keys of my life to You.
You be the driver.
I decide today to let You take the lead.

Thank You, Lord,
For believing in me,
For calling me . . .
        to a noble dream.
A dream to . . .
            Raise children who will love and serve You,
            Leave a legacy of faith in my wake!

I love You, Lord!

                    Amen.

Peanut-Butter Hugs
and Chocolate Kisses

*G*etting Jason to kindergarten on time was a nearly impossible task. Not being graced with the spiritual gift of punctuality, I found it a formidable challenge to get *myself* ready on time, much less three little boys under the age of six. Jason was already at his limit for tardies, and I had a pretty fair idea of what his teacher thought of me — and it wasn't flattering, of that I was sure.

We were required to walk our kindergartners to the classroom door and sign them in. That meant all we mothers were on display as we walked our children in, and our appearance mattered — our hair, our makeup, our hips — not to mention how our children, boys as well as girls, looked — hair painstakingly styled, faces shiny and spotless, clothes carefully assembled to look distinctively alike.

I can't think of anything I endured as a young mother that was more stressful than making my way down the catwalk that wove through the parking lot, along the playground, and past the lunch tables, finally reaching the classroom door, where ultimate judgment awaited: the scrutinizing eyes of the kindergarten teacher. This was a painful daily journey for someone like me who clearly couldn't get her act together.

One day we got to school only to find out that Jason had left his shoes at home. Another day we arrived a half hour late because Christopher had found a mud puddle in the backyard and had completely painted himself in mud — including the insides of his ears. Another morning I put my keys in the pocket of my jacket, then at the last minute threw the jacket in the car, whipping the car door closed, only to realize that I had just locked my keys in the car (it was for people like me that they have since created car doors that cannot be locked unless the key is outside the car)!

The drive on the way to school was equally stressful. Even with Jason (age five), Christopher (age three), and Scotty (age two) all strapped into their own car seats and strategically placed far enough apart to keep them from doing real damage to one another, they could still make faces, throw things, and yell. It required extraordinary focus to keep my eyes off the mirror and on the road, jockeying for position with the other racing minivans in the overcrowded lanes.

It was on one such typical harried morning that I arrived at school with barely a moment to spare. I threw open the side door of the minivan and nearly died when I saw Christopher. He had somehow found gum (don't ask me where, I don't chew the stuff) and on the way to school had smeared it all over his legs, his arms, and even his face. There was no time to go back home and clean him up, so I had no choice but to take him as he was and go sign Jason in. That meant parading another one of my mess-ups in front of all the other mothers, not to mention the teachers.

Struggling to carry two-year-old Scotty on my left hip, hold gummy Christopher with my right hand, and keep an eye on Jason, we walked through the parking lot. As we approached the classrooms, two of the preschool teachers couldn't help but notice my gum-smeared child, so they ran over to give me a helping hand. One of them held Scott, while the second preschool teacher held out a gigantic container of peanut butter. "This works," she assured me. Together we smeared peanut butter all over Christopher's legs, arms, and face. Then we attempted to wipe the peanut butter off with paper towels, but that just created a peanut-butter-gum-paper-towel mixture that covered Chris from head to toe. The teacher's tip didn't work as well as she had led me to believe. The thing is — it didn't bother Christopher that he was such a gummy, peanut-buttery, papery mess. It only bothered me.

Working with children, both as a mother and as an educator, has taught me to approach God like a child. Children don't think to clean themselves up before they play with you or before they run up and throw their arms around you. If they have peanut butter all over their faces or chocolate-covered lips, they will likely give you a peanut-butter hug or a chocolate kiss.

Don't bother to get cleaned up before claiming the mercy of God. It is folly to think we *can* clean ourselves up, and attempting to do so just prolongs the wait to experience God's grace. That's God's job. Not ours. So, come to God as you are. Throw your arms around God no matter how dirty, no matter how ashamed you feel, no matter how messed up you are. Our heavenly Father appreciates the authentic affection inherent in peanut-butter hugs and chocolate kisses from us — the kind of love that feels free to run into His arms without cleaning up first, just as we are—gum, peanut butter, chocolate, dirt, and all.

No matter how messed up you are—don't delay!
Throw your arms around your heavenly Father
And give Him peanut-butter hugs and chocolate kisses!

Create in me a pure heart, O God,
and renew a steadfast spirit within me.

—Psalm 51:10

Heavenly Father —
I made a mess of things . . .

I spoke when I should have been quiet,
I kept still when I should have spoken up,

I withheld affection when I should have reached out,
I interfered when I should have kept my nose out of it.

Now, if I try to clean up the mess, it will only get worse.

So, I run to You and give You the mess.
Redeem it. Clean it up as only You can do!

Thank You for loving me — just as I am — messes and all!

Amen.

When You Crash and Burn—
Grab onto Heavenly Help!

School was out and my boys were waiting for me to pick them up. Waiting in a line of cars with an infant and a four-year-old to pick up Jason from third grade and Chris from first grade was not my idea of fun. My boys were a handful in the car at the best of times, such as when we were moving and the scenery was changing, but when we just had to sit and wait, they became fidgety and usually their choice of entertainment was to annoy each other, which would erupt into chaos, anger, and tears in a matter of seconds.

I had tried the "getting there early" strategy, and that was a mistake. That just meant waiting in line longer than ever! I eventually learned that if I arrived at the last minute the line usually had dwindled to nothing. I could zoom up and the boys could jump in almost without my having to put on the brakes.

Of course, our elementary school was not the only school getting out at this time. The streets were teeming with moms in their minivans, as well as teens in their beefed-up pickup trucks (boys) and compact cars (girls) on their way home, to the store, or to jobs.

It was a typical school day and I was only a few blocks from home. I saw the compact car slowly inching out of the shopping center as if trying to get a better view of the oncoming traffic. But then I felt a huge bump on the back of the van. *She hit me!* I thought angrily (the mother bear in me kicking in). *She wasn't just inching out, she was pulling out, and she hit me! How could she not see a large brown boxy van right in front of her?*

That bump caused the minivan to start spinning wildly. We careened a full 180 degrees until we were facing oncoming traffic. Then, to my horror, the van began to tip! My world spun out of control in slow motion. My sons and I were showered with splintered glass as all the windows simultaneously imploded. *This is it,* I thought. *This is the moment we all fear, and now it is here. Be with us, Lord Jesus!*

We finally came to a stop, resting on my side of the van, my elbow smashed into the pavement, and my sons literally hanging above me strapped from their seats. (This was before air bags, so we were spared the blast of that extra protection.) I was terrified that the glass had torn my sons to shreds. Forcing myself to look, I saw to my relief that Scott was fine. I took a deep breath and hesitantly looked over my shoulder expecting to see the worst. But Nick was also miraculously fine — not a scratch on either of them! At that point, lying on my side with slivers of glass and crunched metal all around us I cried out loud, with tears running down my face, "Thank You, Lord! Thank You, Jesus!"

At this point Scott realized that he should be scared and started to cry.

"It's okay, sweetheart. We're okay," I reassured him.

Then I saw the face of a teenage boy peering in through the

smashed windshield. He had tawny short hair and dark eyebrows. He spoke very slowly and firmly to me, "Turn off your engine."

I was in shock. So he had to repeat it. Very calmly he said again, "Turn—off—your—engine."

Oh, yeah. My engine was still running. Of course. I turned the key in the ignition and the car stopped running.

The young teen gave me another clear instruction: "Unlock—the—door."

As before, he had to repeat my next set of instructions. "Unlock—the—door."

I pressed the unlock button and heard the side door of the van behind me slide open, glass and metal crunching sickeningly. I panicked for a moment as I could hear but not see this stranger lift out Nick, then Scott. Finally, he gave me my last set of instructions: "Here's my hand. Watch your head."

Oh, yeah, you can't stand up in a van that is on its side, I realized. Unbuckling my seat belt, bent over nearly in half, I stepped gingerly on the crunched glass under my feet.

He sat me down on the curb next to my son. Nick was still strapped into his car seat. *What a smart teenager,* I marveled. A woman who introduced herself as a nurse said to me, "You're bleeding." I hadn't felt a thing. She reached into Nick's diaper bag (how did that get there?) and put a diaper on my elbow.

We Colemans had literally stopped traffic. The fire trucks and ambulance closed off the street. My minivan was an unrecognizable mass of twisted metal and shattered glass. I shuddered to look at it and realize that we had all emerged from it unscathed.

The paramedic was impressed with the diaper bandage. "Great idea!" he said, praising the nurse who happened to be there. Another stranger offered to call my husband. She wrote down his number and walked over to the nearby gas station and called him from a pay phone.

They put me on a stretcher and lifted me into the back of the ambulance where my boys were already waiting for me. My entire body was shaking. What had we just survived? As the ambulance, sirens wailing, carried my sons and me past the school where we were supposed to pick up Jason and Christopher, I worried how they'd react when we failed to show up. There was no way to reach them. I could only trust that the school would watch them until Jim could get there. I later learned that my husband passed us on the way to the hospital. He saw the minivan, a crunched-up mess being towed away from the scene. He told me that he was extremely grateful to the young woman who called and prefaced her words with, "Your wife and sons are okay." If he had seen the wreckage without that assurance, he would have feared the worst. As it was he confessed that his first thought was, *What was Sheila doing that she shouldn't have been doing while driving?*

After Jim picked up Jason and Chris from the school's day care, they all bounded into the emergency room where I was getting stitches and Scott's head was being x-rayed because he had smacked it into the window of the minivan. "Mom, you were late picking us up. Where were you? Wow, this is cool!"

Over the years I have repeatedly replayed in my mind what happened to us in the van. I can still see the young teenage boy's face giving me vital instructions through the smashed windshield. But once I got to the curb I never saw him again. For quite some time I wished I could locate him and thank him. But the more I thought about it, the more puzzled I became.

How did he get his face two inches from the windshield? He appeared to be looking straight in at me, but how could that be if we were on our side? Where did he go so quickly? Why didn't he wait and sit with us after all he had done?

I have since become convinced that he was an angel sent from God. Whether he was a human messenger or a spiritual messenger, I know God sent him when we needed God's help. I have since worked with many remarkable teens. But the presence of mind, the clarity of the instructions, transcends anything I have ever witnessed from a teenage boy.

In truth, however, it matters not whether he was a spiritual messenger or a human messenger. What matters is that God cared enough about us to send us help. He was there with us through the entire ordeal. Even though we looked death in the face, there was a peace that can be explained only by the presence of God.

I was helpless, totally inadequate. I had to rely on the help of strangers—people I had never met and whom I have never seen or talked to since. I couldn't think to turn off my engine. I couldn't think to unlock the door. I wouldn't have thought to lift my baby out of the car while strapped in his car seat. I was not enough for my family when they needed me the most. I had literally crashed and burned. But God rescued us with heavenly help! What an awesome, powerful, heavenly reassurance.

I need help! I can't do it myself!
The more I need Him, the stronger He is!
What a heavenly reassurance!

Guard my life and rescue me;
let me not be put to shame,
for I take refuge in you.

— PSALM 25:20

Dear Savior,
I praise You for rescuing me from
>My inadequacies
>My fears
>My futile attempts to make a good impression

When my life spins hideously out of control,
Help me through
>Angels — both human and spiritual
>Who hold my hand
>And bandage my bruised ego

Spare my children and me from
>My well-intentioned mistakes
>My lack of careful attention
>My need to be all they need

Free me to be
>A mother who knows that
>I am all that I need to be
>Because I am trusting in You

To help and rescue me
When I crash and burn

Thank You, Lord!

Amen.

The "Perfect Parent" Trap

🎔 I gave my sons solid foods and stopped nursing them
    sooner than recommended because I wanted to sleep
    through the night.

🎔 I yelled at my boys while getting ready for school.

🎔 I ate half of the leftover birthday cake when no one
    was looking.

🎔 I slept in and missed my devotion time.

🎔 I said no to my husband and fell into bed exhausted.

🎔 I slept on the couch while my boys watched TV.

🎔 I didn't do my exercises.

🎔 I pretended to listen to my husband and my sons but
    couldn't tell you a word they said.

*T*he list goes on and on. It is endless! I have absolutely no
problem thinking of where I have not been the mother
(and wife) I should have been. I feel like the most imperfect
mother in the world.

But I keep *trying* to be perfect! Every day I make a long list
and think, *Today is the day I will be perfect.* And there are some

days when I fall into bed at night and think, *Not perfect, but pretty darn close!*

And there are other days (most, actually) when I look back on my day and think, *I might as well hang it up. There's no use in trying anymore. I am hopelessly imperfect.*

Silly me! Somehow I have believed that if my hair were perfect, my body perfect, my skin perfect, my accomplishments perfect, my cooking, cleaning, and mothering were all perfect, then my family would love me more and my sons would be more successful. Yet, nothing could be farther from the truth! If I were perfect in all those ways — *nobody* would love me. People would resent me and not be able to relate to me — including and especially my family.

So why do I keep trying to be perfect? Because I want to be loved. And somewhere I mistakenly bought into the lie that my imperfections could keep me from being loved. But in truth, this logic is backward, counterintuitive. I have since learned that I can show I care more by being fallible than I can by setting a standard so high that it intimidates others. Then all I have managed to build is a wall, a moat that holds those I love at arm's distance. Ironically, it is my foibles, my wide hips, my face that not only has wrinkles but zits, my dusty house — in short, all my imperfections that draw people closer to me.

Perfection is not only unattainable; it is also undesirable. And the more I try to attain it, the more I will lose out on the true joy of being a mother. The more I strive toward perfection, the more trapped I become by failure and guilt. Trapped by the need to be perfect — I can be freed only with the grace of the cross of Jesus Christ.

Trapped by the need to be a perfect parent —
But Jesus has snapped this trap — and freed me!

In Him we have redemption through His blood,
the forgiveness of our trespasses,
according to the riches of His grace.

— EPHESIANS 1:7 NASB

Beautiful Savior,
Free me from the trap of perfection . . .
Snap the trap . . .
Liberate me
So I can be free . . .
     To be the mother You need me to be
     Imperfect . . . Just as I am . . .
Beautiful flaws that make me
     Unique . . .
     One of a kind . . .
     Accessible
     An example to my children
     And my friends
Of a mother who is free to be imperfect

I praise You for loving me as I am . . .
     Doubts, fears, failures, and all.

I am all I need to be . . .
     Perfected in Your love . . .
     And Your grace!

Amen.

Erasers: Reminders of God's Power and Mercy

A beautiful Christian woman; nevertheless, she was squeamish. As a first-year music teacher, she ran into the office panicky whenever one of her students had a bloody nose or worse. We often giggled and teased her about how she would handle pregnancy.

But Carol surprised us, handling her pregnancy with grace and ease. Athletic, an avid runner, she breezed through her pregnancy while we older, more maternal office personnel watched her maintain her slim hips even as her delivery time drew nearer. How we marveled and celebrated with her at the delivery of her little boy. Would he be an athlete like his handsome father, or have the voice of an angel like his mother?

So I was stunned when Carol dropped by my office one day and said, "Sheila, it's the strangest thing. I had the opportunity to have a free heart test done, so I took it. But it showed that I have a heart condition called cardiomyopathy. The doctors have said I can't have any more children."

I have seen again and again that it matters not how many children a woman has, the abrupt end of any pregnancy, or the news that there will be no more children, is *always* devastating. I searched her face carefully, looking for signs of grief. But Carol's eyes reflected only calm faith as she said, "I am very grateful for my son, Jacob. I really don't need to have any more children. And I am so glad that God was watching out for me by helping the doctors discover this in time to treat it."

But Carol's treatment took its toll. Carol lost her bubbling good spirits. The heart medicine zapped her energy and she found it difficult to do her morning jogs. That was her one complaint, that she wished she could have her energy back. So I encouraged her to share her struggles with the children in her choir. "They can pray for you, Carol."

"But I don't want them to worry."

"Allow them to be a part of your healing. Give them a chance to pray for you."

It took a few months, but Carol did eventually tell her choir what was going on, and in true fashion, the children began to pray. They prayed for God to heal their beloved teacher's heart. And miracle of miracles, a year later, Carol came bursting into the office. "The cardiologist can't believe it! He said that my heart is healed. He can't explain it, but I don't have to be on heart medication any longer."

What a testimony this was to all of us and to the children who had prayed!

But the story didn't end there. When Jacob was two and a half, he came down with a rare illness, Kawasaki disease. The residual effect of this disease was also rare. Jacob's left coronary artery was left with several extremely large aneurisms. Carol and Dave listened in disbelief as the doctors broke the news that there was no cure, no surgery, no way to treat this condition except with blood thinners to prevent blood clots. Yet, to look at this precious towhead tear through the hospital corridors on the hospital tricycle, it was difficult to imagine that a time bomb was ticking in his heart.

The blood thinners proved difficult to manage. At times Jacob bit his tongue, or he started to bleed in his throat. Then Carol rushed him to emergency where they reversed the blood thinning long enough to stanch the bleeding, then resumed blood thinners until the next episode. This went on for about a year. Then one day the doctors pronounced that Jacob's aneurisms were getting better and he could stop taking the blood thinners.

Carol was thrilled. It seemed that God had once again performed a heart miracle in the young Aspling family. But ultimately it was determined that the aneurisms were still there. And because Jacob had stopped taking blood thinners, a blood clot had formed at a particularly dangerous spot on one of the weak aneurisms on his coronary artery.

Her faith sustaining her, Carol told her choir about Jacob's turn for the worse, but in her unique and amazing way she said, "If God can erase our sins, how much easier is it for Him to erase one tiny clot in Jacob's heart?"

What Carol told the children made its way back to my office. We were only days from a large benefit concert scheduled in the Crystal Cathedral. I knew nearly a thousand people would be there that night, and Carol's choir was a large part of the concert.

So I asked my assistant to purchase a thousand new Pink Pearl erasers. I asked the ushers to fill the offering plates with the erasers. I told everyone that it was a surprise. The night of the concert, at the very end, after the choir had finished singing, the audience was told about Jacob and asked to pray for him. "Everyone who is willing to commit to praying that God will erase the clot in Jacob's heart, please come and get an eraser."

For the first time I saw Carol cry as hundreds of people and all of the children from her choir filed down and took erasers. We closed in prayer for Jacob, and in the days that followed, erasers with Jacob's name etched on them could be found throughout the school, on children's desks, teachers' desks, and office desks.

So it came as no surprise when at Jacob's next checkup the same cardiologist said to Carol, "I don't know what you are doing, but keep it up. First your heart and now Jacob's. His clot is gone!"

Carol told Jacob, then five, that they no longer needed their family eraser, but as she went to throw it away, Jacob challenged her: "But Mom, the Israelites kept their clay manna jars to remind them of the faithfulness of God! So shouldn't we keep our erasers to remind us of the faithfulness of God?" (See Exod. 16:33.)

What a gift this young mother has given to her child and the children in her choir: the gift of grace and the gift of faith. These two gifts go hand in hand, as Carol taught all of us!

God's grace is big enough to erase our sins!
His power is big enough to carry us through
Our toughest times!

The LORD is my strength and my song;
he has become my salvation.
He is my God, and I will praise him.

—EXODUS 15:2

Almighty God,
Heavenly Father,
Gracious Savior,

You have the power to . . .
        Erase my sins . . .
        Heal me from my mistakes . . .
        Save me from my weaknesses.

You have the power to . . .
Carry me through anything!
Even when my children are threatened . . .
        By illness
        Or rejection
        Or failure . . .
Ultimately, they are Your children!
And You will see me — and them
Through even the most trying times!

Amen.

Broken Marriage: Broken Mom?

She sat in my office, crying. Her husband had asked for a divorce. Liz,* who had three children, was suddenly, and against her wishes, facing the reality of living life as a single mother. I refrained from trying to rescue her and merely handed her a tissue. How could I possibly help her, when I had never walked in her shoes? I could not say, "I understand." And truth be told, I was worried about the children. How would they fare now that their world had been torn asunder?

"What are you going to do?" I asked simply.

"I'm not going to fight him for it."

"What about the children?"

"I suppose he'll want to share custody. He loves the kids."

"Well, you will grieve, no doubt about it. This is a death — the death of a dream."

At a loss for words, she buried her head in her hands and sobbed. "I never saw it coming."

* "Liz" represents a compilation of many mothers with this issue who have sat in my office. My responses in the dialogue presented here are, in essence, what I told each and every one of them.

"Just know we are here for you. Feel free to come in any-time you need a shoulder."

As a school administrator, I was glad to be informed about what was happening at home. It helped the staff and me in the days to come when the kids displayed some symptoms that home was being reframed and family was being redefined. The transition took its toll, but the brokenhearted mother came in from time to time and I would listen.

"Dr. Coleman, I worry about the kids. I am so angry at their father! And I feel like a broken woman."

"The good news is that God specializes in putting the pieces of our lives back together. Situations like this are always hard on everyone, especially the kids, but there are things you can do to keep the damage to a minimum. I have seen many, many children come through this school who are from broken homes. And I can tell you which homes are still broken, and which ones are making it work, just by the kids' behavior."

"What's the difference?"

"The difference is something very simple, but incredibly diffi-cult to do—especially on a consistent basis. The price is steep, but the payoff is priceless. The difference is this: the parents who con-tinue to work together, agreeing on child-raising principles such as homework and discipline, as well as refraining from bad-mouthing their spouses in front of the children—those are the homes where the kids come through—stronger at the broken places."

"Oh. I don't think I can do that. He hurt me so much, I can't help myself. I—"

"I'm not saying you have to stop feeling angry at him. Just don't express those feelings in front of the kids. He is their father, after all. Anything negative you say about him will leave them ashamed of their father, and that will affect their self-esteem. So, go ahead and be angry, just find someone else to vent with—a friend, your mother, me—anyone but the kids."

"I can do that."

"It will take time, but with counseling [which I always suggest for people going through something like this], you and your kids can come out whole on the other side of this."

"You promise?"

"Some of the best mothers I know are single. Some have lost their husbands through divorce, others through death. There is no question that their lives are harder than mine. They have to do the work of two parents with no one to give them a break. It can be exhausting. But I have seen that the children who come from broken homes and homes parented by only a single mother can turn out just as well-adjusted, just as productive, just as loving as children from happy, two-parent homes."

I took a breath. She was listening intently, so I pressed on. "Broken homes don't have to equate with a broken mother and hence broken kids. But the work, the effort, the challenges for single moms are more than twice as hard as they are for mothers who have spouses."

"So we can get through this?"

"You can! Just remember to work with your ex and not against him for the kids' sake. And be sure to be good to yourself. The more whole you are, the more whole your kids will be. That means taking time for yourself, treating yourself—even keeping Hershey's Kisses in your desk drawer—and not being too hard on yourself."

"Is there anything else I can do to help my kids through this?"

"Well, it's common knowledge that kids think divorce is their fault. If they had been better at home or at school, Dad would have stayed. You can continually remind them that this is not their fault. The same goes for you. It won't help anybody for you to keep beating yourself up, second-guessing something you should have done more of or less of.

"The moms who can put their lives back together are the ones whose kids make it. The only way I can think of for you to do that is through the help of Jesus. Let Him heal you and make you whole again. Allow yourself to accept His love and forgiveness. Don't push Him away just because your husband was a jerk. I've seen too many women do that. They blame God as well as their husbands. You need Jesus more than ever right now."

"But I'm ashamed."

"Of what?"

"How could I have picked him in the first place?"

"Would you turn back the clock and not marry him if you knew this would happen?"

"Of course!"

"But then you wouldn't have your precious children. Would you choose your children or to be spared your pain?"

"My children."

"Focus on them now. They are the silver lining, the redeeming element. In time you will see that they make even this pain worth it."

Broken marriage does not necessarily mean
Broken mom or broken kids
When
God is allowed to pick up the pieces!

The LORD is close to the brokenhearted
and saves those who are crushed in spirit.

—PSALM 34:18

Dear Lord,
I have never walked their painful road,
But I have seen their agony,
Heard their anger,
Felt their pain.

Carry them when
>The load gets too heavy
>The road gets too confusing
>The pain gets to be too much to bear

Life's not fair,
But You are good
So I implore You
>To intervene
>To heal
>To mend
>To put back the pieces
>To make them whole again

Help them to see
That they can still be
    Awe-some mothers
    Whole-some mommies!

        Amen.

Even Good Mothers
(and Heavenly Fathers)
Have Kids Who Make
Poor Choices

*T*he preschool director was making her rounds through the classrooms. One little girl excitedly tugged on her skirt and said, "Come see what I made!"

The director walked over to where Laini had built an "ark" out of blocks. She had assembled a parade of small plastic animals marching two-by-two into the ark. On the other side of the ark were rows of toy people lying facedown.

"See, it's Noah's ark! Here are the animals. And see those dead people over there? They are the ones who made poor choices!"

When kids in school make poor choices they end up not lying facedown on the floor, but rather sitting in the principal's office. I have learned that even apparently innocent little angels can be guilty of making poor choices. But getting them to admit to making those poor choices can be a challenge.

One day two students were in the office, feeling under the weather and resting on cots. Suddenly one of them came running into my office, saying, "Mrs. Coleman, Sharon bit me!" (The names are changed to protect the innocent and, in this case, the guilty, also.)

Sharon, the accused, was one of our brightest and best students with a track record of exemplary behavior. The victim, Natalie, was known for being a less-than-model student.

I called Sharon in and said, "Natalie says you bit her. Did you?"

Sharon innocently replied, "No, Mrs. Coleman, I did not bite her."

Great! One child's word against another's. I just love these situations! Whom to believe — the one with the angelic reputation or the one with the tarnished past? I was tempted to believe that Sharon was innocent and that Natalie was making up another one of her stories, maybe this time out of jealousy.

It was my job to make sure I found out the truth — and not just jump to convenient conclusions. What if Natalie was telling the truth? If so, and I dismissed her story based on her reputation, then I would be doing her a disservice and reinforcing the belief that she was untrustworthy. Also, Sharon would be getting away with something she needed to account for, and that was not the lesson I wanted her to learn.

So, I decided to give the conflict my full attention and dove into it with the investigative skills one learns on a job like mine. It took most of my day, talking to both of the girls separately, then together, then separately again. I wish I could recall what triggered the confession, but after a few hours of going back and forth, Sharon suddenly spilled the beans: "I did it, Mrs. Coleman. I don't know why. Her hand was just there, near my mouth, and before I knew it, I just bit her for no good reason." Tears began to slide down her cheeks. "I am so sorry."

I learned that even angelic little girls make poor choices! And when our children make poor choices — then what? As we teach our children the importance of making good choices, we are faced with also teaching them the message of grace when they make poor choices. And the same is true for us mothers (and churches). Too often as I have worked in ministry, I have seen parents run away from the church when their kids started making poor choices, instead of running toward the church for support and encouragement. Too often I have watched mothers hear the message that if they do a good enough job raising their children, praying for them, keeping them in church, and reading the Bible to them, their children will make good choices throughout their lives. In other words—how our children turn out depends on us!

What a horrendous burden to put on parents. Especially since we know it is much more complicated than that!

Imagine if a family in your church had a child who became enmeshed in drug abuse. What is the first thing we all think? *What did the parents do wrong? What did they fail to do? Or what are they guilty of doing?* Well, it's rarely that simple. Usually it is a complicated combination of influences, both external (nurture) and internal (nature), that determines how our children turn out. Yet, we parents live under the heavy and unreasonable weight of thinking we have the power to prevent our children from hurting others or themselves through poor choices. Although there are many steps you can take to minimize the risks and maximize the chances that your child will make good choices in life, the reality is that there are no absolute guarantees, no magic formulas.

If that were the case, wouldn't God have used them to ensure that *His* children were immune from making poor choices? Yet, He created all of His children with the ability to choose, and consequently, He knew that we *all* make poor choices from time to time. That meant He himself chose to provide a way for His beloved children to be forgiven for whatever poor choices they would make — by sending His Son, Jesus Christ.

In the final analysis, we moms can be held responsible only for our own choices — not our children's. We can find our own forgiveness only in our Lord. So, when your children make poor choices — and Scripture tells us they all will — remember that even God's children make poor choices — all the time. The choices your children make are not a reflection that you have been a poor mother. You now have another choice — how you will respond to their poor choices. I highly suggest following the example of Jesus and how He responds to us when we make our poor choices — a response of love and forgiveness.

Make the good choice —
The God choice —
To love and forgive ourselves —
And those we love —
Anyway!

We love because he first loved us.

— 1 JOHN 4:19

Heavenly Father,
I choose today to believe in You
And to accept Your grace for me.
I choose today to believe . . .
      That I am a good mother
      That the choices my children make
Are not my fault . . .
Nor are they my credit.

Thank You, heavenly Father
For giving us, Your children
The freedom to make choices . . .
      Even if it means making poor choices
And thank You for forgiving
And loving us . . . Anyway!

Amen!

Sorry Seems to Be
the Hardest Word

*I*t was opening day for Little League. Jim had taken two of the boys, and I was supposed to meet him with the other two at the ballpark. Due to the complicated schedule of the day (they were in a performing choir and took trumpet and trombone lessons, so Saturdays usually required the tactical skills of an air traffic controller), we needed two vehicles. As team mother I was expected to head the snack shack that day.

After rounding up the myriad uniform pieces for three of the four boys (Nick, at four years of age, was too young to play), I dashed out of the house — late as usual. The park was fifteen minutes from home, high on a windy hill overlooking the city. It was a beautiful sunny California spring day. The park was teeming with young families with boys in sparkling clean uniforms. That, I knew from previous years, would be a brief sight. By the end of the day, they would be covered in red clay and grass stains.

It took some time for me to get the snack shack up and running, but eventually I had time to break away and see how my sons' opening games were going. I crossed the large expanse of park that housed six baseball fields, looking for my husband. Spotting him, I ran up to him and said, "Hi, hon! How're the games going?"

"They haven't started yet. Jason's team is warmed up and they are just about to start. The other games don't start for another hour."

"Where's Nicky?"

"Nicky? I don't have Nicky. You have Nicky."

"Me? No, I don't! You have him, don't you . . . ?"

Suddenly we looked at each other in horror as the realization of what we had done hit us. "He's home alone! My gosh, he's been there for over an hour all alone!"

Jim ran to the car. It would take him another fifteen minutes to get home. I couldn't believe that we had made such a terrible mistake! My poor baby!

When he drove into the driveway and went around to the back, he saw Nick wandering around the backyard, his hands cupped to the windows. Locked out, he looked longingly into his house. He was muttering to himself, "I can't believe they left me home alone."

Jim swept him up into his arms. "I'm home, Nick! I came back for you!"

"Daddy! You left me home alone!"

"It was a mistake—all a mistake. Mom thought you went with me and I thought you were with her. Are you all right?"

"Yes. I knew you'd come back for me."

What a welcome sight to see him come running across the field with his father a half hour later! "Nick!" I grabbed him and hugged him tightly. I felt so guilty I could hardly look him in the eyes.

"You left me home alone!" he scolded.

"Yes." I gulped and looked him squarely in those accusing blue eyes, knowing I had to say those two little words, the two hardest words in the world — those words that verify to all who hear them that I'm less than I should be — "I'm sorry!"

He looked at me, searching my face for authenticity. Finding what he was looking for, his face broke into a smile. "That's okay, I forgive you!"

Whew! What a relief — he was safe and sound — *and* he forgave me.

~~~~~~

It's easy to make mistakes
It's hard to say, "I'm sorry."
But these words teach our children the
Really important lesson:
That we all need to forgive and be forgiven!

~~~~~~

He who conceals his sins does not prosper,
but whoever confesses and renounces them finds mercy.

—PROVERBS 28:13

Lord Jesus Christ,
Thank You for teaching me the power of saying,
"I'm sorry."

Why is it so hard to admit
      That I made a mistake
      That I'm not perfect
      That I need help

Yet, those two little words
Those damning little words
That prove I am fallible
Are the key to
      Learning lessons and
      Teaching lessons

Lessons that
      Heal
      Repair breaches
      Build bridges

Give me the courage
      To admit when I've been wrong

To confess when I've messed up
To repent when I've been hurtful

"I'm sorry" for not paying enough attention.
"I'm sorry" for being too harsh.
"I'm sorry" for losing my temper.

Thank You for forgiving me and loving me!

Amen.

Love Covers a Multitude of Sins

$\mathcal{M}$y excuse for my inexcusable behavior is that my husband had pneumonia and was in bed for nearly two months, leaving me vulnerable to the wiles of my four resourceful and mischievous sons. I was at the end of my rope. My patience with being a single mother of four boys under the age of ten had reached its limits long before. I was bone weary. Not a nurturing woman, even in the best of circumstances, I was tired of running up and down the stairs trying to take care of my sick, sick husband.

When we first got married Jim pleaded for a two-story house. "I don't want to run up and down stairs taking care of you when you get sick," I protested.

"Don't worry. I'll be sick downstairs."

The first time Jim got sick he rang a bell for me from the second-floor bedroom. Hands on hips, I glared at him unsympathetically and asked, "What happened to being sick downstairs?"

"I'm too sick for downstairs. I'm upstairs sick."

And so for the rest of our married life, Jim has been upstairs sick. When he was sick with pneumonia, he really was upstairs sick, and I did not mind bringing him all he needed, but there was no time for me to sit and hold his hand. I would rush into the bedroom, hurriedly drop off his dinner on a tray, give him a hasty kiss on his warm forehead, and rush back downstairs to complete pandemonium.

My situation was worsened by the fact that as a parent, I had played the good cop to Jim's bad cop. I learned much later how to balance this, but at the time of his illness, the boys knew they could manipulate me, but not their father. After a month of struggling to keep the house running with even a semblance of order, I faced a chaotic dinner during which the boys refused to listen.

"Stop!" I ordered.

Nothing.

"Stop!" I ordered louder.

They continued as if I weren't even in the room.

"Stop!" I shouted. "Or I'll . . ."

The chaos continued unabated.

"I'll take you to the home."

This was met with silence. Curious faces looked up at me. "What home?"

"The home for boys who won't listen to their mothers."

"You wouldn't do that!"

"Yes, I would."

I was digging myself in deeper and deeper. My threat was going unheeded. The boys were challenging me, so I felt that I had no choice but to follow through. (I later learned that you should never threaten unless you can carry it through. I still had so much to learn as a mother!)

They continued to ignore me even with this new threat. So I declared, "That's it! All of you — get into the car at once. I am taking you to the boys' home!"

Finally, they seemed to get the message. It amazes me to look back on this and think that I seriously thought I was doing the right or wise thing. My only conclusion is that I was too frazzled to think. For it is obvious to me today that I wasn't thinking — at all — just reacting out of sheer desperation!

"Get in the car! All of you!"

Scott, just four years old, began to cry. "I don't want to go to the home."

"Too late! You should have thought of that sooner!"

I piled all of them in the car. It was dark out. Jason and Christopher goaded, "There's no home for boys."

"There is! I'll prove it!"

I drove around for several miles, trying to get them scared enough to listen and obey me. Finally, I pulled into a dark, empty lot of an industrial center.

"Here we are! Get out!"

Scott began to wail, but Jason was old enough to not be fooled.

"This isn't a home! This is just a stupid carpet factory!"

Defeated, I gave up. Scott's tears tore at me, and I actually stopped and thought about what I was doing. But rather than apologize (as I should have done), I said, "All right. You can come back home with me. But if you don't start listening to me, I will find a boys' home for real!"

As a trained educator today, I can hardly write this story without wincing in shame. Fear of abandonment does nothing to instill confidence, trust, or healthy self-esteem in a child.

And needless to say, it was completely ineffective as a disciplinary tool.

After we returned home, and I had somehow managed to get them all into bed, I finally took time to think about what I had done. Thoroughly ashamed, I vowed nobody would ever hear about this horrendous mothering of mine.

Although my mother-in-law promised me that the boys would not remember times such as this that I wanted them to forget, they not only remember it, they relish replaying it whenever guests are seated around the table. The one incident of which I am the most ashamed as a mother, is *the* story they tell over and over again. The first time they repeated the story in horrific detail to friends who had come over for dinner, I thought I would die of embarrassment. I slid lower and lower into my chair. I glared at them with my most menacing look, but as usual, they ignored my threats and continued to tell the story, taking great glee in my worst moment ever.

The "carpet factory" story is now legend and is still told, the boys always laughing uproariously. But the incident has transformed over the years from a moment of shame to a moment of family bonding. The negative overtones of the incident have, over the years and with each retelling, diminished for me — primarily because today it is obvious that my horrendous blunder did not have negative effects on them after all. Somehow, they still turned out to be fine young men — in spite of my shortcomings.

If only I had known more about parenting. If only I hadn't been too proud to take parenting classes. If only I had known more about discipline. If only I had been a teacher first, and a mother second. If only . . . what? Would they have turned out any better than they have? No!

I did the best I could at the time. I made mistakes — to be sure! But my sons knew — even when I threatened to take them to the carpet factory — that I loved them. I suspect that is why the ploy never worked and why they find it so amusing today. I was totally unbelievable! As a professional educator I know it is impossible to fool children. They can always see through to the truth. And in my case, the truth was, and is, that I love them madly! My love for them — and their love for me — and the cross of Jesus Christ — mercifully covers a multitude of my sins!

The love of Christ covers a multitude of sins!

Have mercy upon me, O God,
According to Your lovingkindness;
According to the multitude of Your tender mercies,
Blot out my transgressions.
Wash me thoroughly from my iniquity,
And cleanse me from my sin.

—PSALM 51:1–2 NKJV

Lord,
How could I have been so foolish?
What in the world was I thinking?
I suppose that's the problem . . .
I wasn't thinking, just reacting
And in the process I got myself caught up in a power
　　　struggle
With my sons . . . with myself.

The next time I forget to use my head,
Give me the grace to *think* —
　　　　Why I am doing what I am doing . . .
　　　　And saying what I am saying.

And when I can't stop myself
From making a mess of things
Give me the grace to *know* —
　　　　That I have been forgiven . . .
　　　　And You can clean up my mess for me!

I do not have to earn my atonement!

I do not have to scrub away the marred emotions!

I do not have to earn back the respect and admiration!

I have merely to reach out and take the free gift of Your
      salvation!

Thank You, Lord!

Amen.

Making a Mess of
Things — Again!

I don't know whose idea it was to buy the ivory velour love seat that sat smack-dab in the middle of the family room, but it *was* my idea to have it Scotchgarded! This was the chair the boys loved to plop down in to watch *Sesame Street* while I tossed all the toys into the toy box, got dinner on the table, and gave Jim the false impression that I had it all together.

But days with no school were a challenge. Trying to keep the boys involved in constructive as opposed to destructive (of things or one another) activities kept me on my toes. In the process, most of the time we ended up making a huge mess. The day we attempted to make a gingerbread village was one of the worst. Jason's clock tower turned out really beautiful. He had painstakingly used royal icing, a frosting that hardens like glue as it dries, to attach silver beads outlining the tower and even used the beads to indicate the numbers on the face of the clock. But when I went to place it in the kitchen window, I accidentally nicked the top of the delicate creation under the bottom of the cupboard, which shattered the clock into a zillion pieces and sent the silver beads rolling all over the kitchen floor.

"Oh, Mom!" Jason cried.

"We can fix it," I lied.

We actually had to reassemble most of it from scratch, but together, with our heads buried in the task, we rebuilt the tower. It was the crowning touch—Jason's clock tower—to our gingerbread village in the window. "Whew!" I took a deep breath. But I knew that now I was running woefully behind schedule and it would take some time to clean up the mess before Jim got home.

I indulged in one last proud look at the village before facing the messy kitchen. I had been so engrossed (focused to a fault) in helping Jason fix his tower that I had not noticed that Christopher had been painting the back of the sofa with the leftover frosting *and* a black marker. The entire back of the sofa, which was the first thing you saw when you entered the family room, was covered with black marker and white frosting! This was in addition to the kitchen table covered with dirty bowls and graham cracker crumbs, the floor sticky from frosting, and the counters covered with powdered sugar boxes, mixing spoons, and bags and bags of candy.

I glanced at the clock—Jim was due home in less than an hour!

Thank heaven for *Sesame Street*. I switched on the TV and plopped the boys down and began to scrub and mop and hurl dishes into the sink. How could I have made such a mess—not to mention the couch! I took a bowl of water and some old towels and began to work on the back of the couch. I was sure it was ruined. What would Jim say? What would he think? But wonder of wonders, the frosting dissolved in the water and eventually the couch became less sticky. Amazingly, the marker also began to come out. I never would have guessed it, but when I was finished, the couch looked as good as new — though it was very wet. I ran upstairs and got the hair dryer and had just finished drying the couch when I heard the garage door open. I had made it — barely!

Until now, Jim never knew that I had let things get so out of control. Even though I suspect that he was aware I was barely in control of the boys, Jim and I both pretended that I was doing a better job than I really was at managing them.

At the time it seemed so important to feel — to appear — as though I had it all together. Now I realize how silly I was. In retrospect I see that even though we made our fair share of messes, messy times went hand in hand with making the memories we treasure the most. Being a mom is not for the purist. It is messy work. It means getting your hands (and couches) dirty.

I wonder if the same can't be said of our relationship with God. If we go through life trying to keep everything together, afraid to make a mess, we can miss out on the fun, the wonder, the adventure of life. It is only when we dare to make a mess that we truly live, and it is only when we truly live that our faith has a chance to grow. Nothing worth doing is ever easy, and so we can expect to make messes. In fact, messes can be a sign that we are not holding back — on our families, on ourselves, or on our God.

Messes are nothing more than
The by-product of living life abundantly!

The grace of our Lord was poured out on me abundantly,
along with the faith and love that are in Christ Jesus.

— 1 Timothy 1:14

I came that [you] may have life,
and have it abundantly.

— John 10:10 nasb

Jesus, Lord and Savior,
How wonderful, how awesome You are.

Grant me the courage to live life
        Abundantly
        Jumping into the adventure
        Regardless of how messy it might become

Free me from the need to appear
        To have it all together
        Pure
        Clean

Rather, let me jump into life
        With both feet
        With a sense of abandonment
        With the thrill of adventure

Help me to appreciate the enjoyment
Of a full, abundant, messy life!
Knowing that not all messes
    Are to be avoided
Some messes, like our children, like us, Your children,
    Are to be embraced
Resting on the assurance that Your grace is
    Amazing and
    Abundant

       Amen.

Terms of Endearment

*A*s a school principal, most days I deal with children who have misbehaved. And most of the time, when the children sit across from me at my desk, they are very penitent (or at least scared because they know I will call Mom or Dad) for what they have done. It might come as a surprise, but usually I am not angry at them. Quite the contrary: I often have a hard time keeping a straight face when the students are sent to me. Their forthright, comical responses are frequently more amusing than concerning.

Kevin (as before, the names in this story are changed to protect the guilty and the innocent) had been sent to me for some minor infraction, but this was not the first time. Because it was an ongoing problem, he knew he would really be in big trouble at home. When I asked him about the misbehavior, he denied it, saying, "You can go ask Sam. He'll tell you I didn't do it."

So I called in Sam. But Sam said Kevin *did* do it.

Kevin continued to plead his case. "You can ask Ricky. He'll tell you I didn't do it."

I called in Ricky. But Ricky also said that Kevin did do it.

This went on for seven friends, who all testified that Kevin was guilty as charged. So I gave Kevin the news.

At this point, large wet tears began to stream down his face and he protested with as much sincerity and vehemence as a ten-year-old boy can muster, "But Mrs. Coleman! It's my body and I should know if I did it or not!"

I knew I could not smile. If I did, students like Kevin would think their behavior was cute, and that would be the wrong message. As a result, in situations such as this, I frequently have to force my face to look stern or even pretend to look for something in my file drawer to hide my mirth. It is also critical that the student being disciplined not see how lightly I take their mischief for fear that they will misinterpret my emotion. After all, they are usually in tears, and they could easily think I was laughing at them when in fact I find them endearing. So at the end of the day it has been common to find wadded-up tissue bits from their tears on the floor in front of my desk.

My sons were not always sons of a principal. In their early years, before I decided to become a teacher, they went to schools where other principals had the unpleasant chore of calling to tell me something one of my sons had done to earn detention, or worse. Mortified, I was afraid to face the principal in the days that followed. *What must he or she think of me as a mother?* I wondered. *What must he or she think of my son?* I was sure we had lost their respect and even their affection.

I suspect the parents at my school must have had similar feelings. But, truth be told, my affection for children who have been sent to me for making bad choices has not been diminished one iota. Rather than being angry at them, or losing respect or affection for them, I found them all the more endearing.

Imagine my surprise when I first encountered those surprising feelings. That day, as I sat across the desk from Kevin, valiantly attempting to suppress my mirth, even while feeling such affection for him, it occurred to me that perhaps God finds me just as endearing—even when I make poor choices as a mother. Could it be, when I fall flat on my face, that rather than losing face in His eyes, He sees me as His adored daughter? In fact, I wonder how many times my heavenly Father has looked down at me and had to hide a smile, shaking His head. "There she goes again! Will she never learn?"

The truth is that we will never learn. We will make mistake after mistake, even at times (horror of horrors) causing irreparable damage. But even as the scratches on some of my favorite furniture and the chips on some of my china can never be repaired, the marks left behind have over time become reminders of precious memories and undeserved grace. Mercy doesn't always erase the mistake, but it always redeems it, and in the process erases the guilt.

No matter how hard I try, I will never be the perfect mother. That's where the cross of Christ comes in. And somehow it helps to know that even as my children cannot lose my love because they mess up (indeed, they are that much more endearing to me), so I cannot lose my heavenly Father's love, even though I fail where it counts the most—as a mother. He finds me endearing—even when I am an imperfect mother—because He is my heavenly Father.

Thanks to the Cross:
The terms of endearment are never severed—
Even when we sin!

The Lord is slow to anger,
abounding in love and forgiving sin and rebellion.
—Numbers 14:18

Lord,
I did it again!
I lost my temper . . .
I became impatient . . .
I yelled and got angry . . .

When I think of myself
I do not like what I am and
I'm even ashamed.

Nevertheless,
Wonder of wonders,
You find me endearing,
Lovely,
A beautiful mother.

Thank You for the Cross,
Which redeems me.
Help me to see myself today
As You see me — Your precious, endearing child!

Amen.

Better Than a Time Machine

*I*magine being the principal of a school where three of your sons are students! Most people felt sorry for my sons having to be the principal's kids, but I have to say that I frequently felt sorry for myself, having to be the principal where my sons went to school . . . especially the time Nicholas decided to moon one of the female students.

It was at the height of sexual harassment talk on the news. Workplaces and schools were being sued for sexual harassment, and I had gone to all of the training and instructed my staff accordingly. I was conducting a teachers' meeting after school when my administrative assistant tapped on the window of the classroom door.

I shook my head no. I was right in the middle of some very important point. She should have known better than to interrupt.

She tapped again. When I shook my head no, she came in and whispered, "You have to adjourn this meeting. It's about Nick."

Puzzled, I told the teachers I was needed immediately in the office and that our agenda would have to wait. Of course, all of the teachers were more than thrilled to get to go home early.

But my heart was racing as I followed my assistant back to my office. Nick was in fourth grade at the time. He was known and loved for his vibrant personality, intelligent, keen mind, and talent as a performer. "What happened to Nick?"

Carla whispered to me, "He mooned Debbie Pitcher" (name is changed here to protect the innocent, and *only* the innocent).

"He did *what?*"

"He —"

"Don't say it again." I was sure I would be fired, sued, or both.

My son sat in my office across from my desk.

"Nicholas Sean Coleman, what in the world were you thinking?"

"Well, Mom, I asked her if she wanted a full moon or a half-moon. When she didn't answer, I assumed she wanted a full moon. So, that's what I gave her."

Oh, the horrors of being the mother of four sons! What were his big brothers teaching him when I wasn't looking?

"Well, you will have to be suspended immediately. And you will have to write an apology letter to Debbie, and then you will have to take that birthday money you just got and you will go out tonight and buy something beautiful for Debbie so that she will think of something lovely instead of your bare . . . Oh, how could you do this?"

"I'm sorry, Mom." He looked down guiltily, and then, with as much sincerity as a talented actor can muster, he muttered, "In fact, I wish I had a time machine."

"A time machine?"

"Yes, then I could go back in time and do it all different. Then it would be as if I had never mooned Debbie Pitcher."

The good news is that Debbie's mother was very understanding. I admit I avoided her until one day we were both waiting, just the two of us, outside the classroom. I knew I had to apologize to her but was so embarrassed. I finally, timidly said, "Mrs. Pitcher . . . Hi . . . um . . . Thank you for being so understanding about Nicholas. Um . . . I hope the gift gave Debbie something else to think about. . . ."

"Yes, but she did say to me, 'Oh, Mom, every time I think about . . .' and then she shuddered."

I hung my head and said, "I can't tell you how sorry I am."

"Forget it," she mumbled.

As much as I have tried to forget the incident, I have found there is so much truth in Nick's wish for a time machine. Wouldn't all of us love to have a time machine for something we did that was humiliating or hurtful to others or ourselves? What would we give to have a chance to go back in time and undo it?

The good news is that even though we don't have a time machine, we have something better—we have a Savior! Jesus died for our mistakes. That is wonderful news! He died for *all* mistakes, even the ones we make and tear ourselves up over with guilt, guilt, and more guilt. Jesus can help us learn from our mistakes and turn our scars into stars. He can redeem us and make us new. We have a God who not only believes in us—He forgives us.

Jesus is better than a time machine—
He turns my scars into stars—
My mistakes into miracles.

If anyone is in Christ,

he is a new creation;

the old has gone, the new has come!

— 2 Corinthians 5:17

Jesus,

There are words I would take back if I could

Actions I would undo, if I had the ability to turn back time,

But I have the gift of redemption

My mistakes can be turned into miracles

With Your help and Your grace.

Make me new, reborn, the old erased and graced.

Amen.

Love and Discipline:
Finding the Right Balance

*P*ick up those toys, now!" My husband had asked twice before, and with each request, his voice got louder. I knew I did the same thing. It occurred to me that the boys responded only when our voices were at a certain decibel level. They had come to understand that a certain tone and volume indicated when to take us seriously.

Nevertheless, I cringed at Jim's tone and went into my typical rescue mode and began to pick up the toys with them. "It's okay," I reassured my sons. I felt Jim was expecting too much from them, and so I thought if I compensated, they wouldn't rebel or resent us when they got older. I didn't want them to resent Jim, but I for sure didn't want them to resent *me*. I was guilty of saying, "Wait until your father gets home!"

It actually occurred to me more than once that I was not being fair to Jim, but I couldn't seem to help myself. I was a wuss of a mom. I was afraid to discipline the boys for fear they wouldn't love me. And when I did discipline them I felt enormous guilt afterward.

My weakness as a disciplinarian was verified when I left my

classroom as a teacher to be a principal at another school site. As I said my final good-byes to the children in my fifth-grade classroom, one of the boys actually said to me, "Gee, Mrs. Coleman, you're going to be a principal? Wait until the kids at your new school find out you're a marshmallow!"

The image of the marshmallow-puff ghost in *Ghostbusters* immediately popped into my mind. If that image alone didn't strike terror in me, my weakness as a disciplinarian was further reinforced by the teachers at the new school. The teachers I would be managing had known me as a mother since my boys were students there. And the word on the street was that they were afraid I would be too lenient as a principal. Consequently, the agenda of every teachers' meeting for the first year focused on their topic of concern — discipline (or the lack thereof).

Not only was I a wuss when it came to discipline, I was and still am someone who innately avoids conflict and loathes fighting. As a child I became accustomed to being sent home from school sick to my stomach because two little boys had gotten into a playground fight. Even today I can't stand to go to sporting events for fear that the fans will start to push and shove or, heaven forbid, do something worse!

So, what was God thinking, giving me four boys who fought all the time and a school where my job is to pass judgment on playground fights? What was God thinking putting a wuss in charge of discipline? In retrospect, I now see that it was this very adverse reaction I have to fighting and my fear of being a marshmallow that propelled me to become the firm disciplinarian I am at school.

As I tackled the challenge of developing a school-wide discipline plan, I focused on the root word of discipline: *disciple*.

I decided that our goal would be to discipline with the same principle Jesus used to discipline His disciples, which was, more often than not, loving correction combined with teaching. And as I learned to enforce the plan, which included strong consequences for students who fought or hurt someone, I learned finally to find that magical balance between love and discipline. Every time children sit before me requiring discipline, I explain that they can turn this negative into a positive if they learn something from it. I also reassure them that since they have been penitent (if they have been—not all of them are), they will be loved and forgiven at this school.

It is because I desperately seek harmony that I confront conflict (between students, teachers, and parents alike) head-on. It is because I am terrified of school fights that I make sure everyone, especially the students, knows I will tolerate no fighting. As a result, much to my surprise, the very few incidents we've had have all been minor.

Another benefit of discovering I didn't have to be a marshmallow, but could be fair and firm and loving all at the same time, was that this transformation in me carried over into our home. I found myself in principal mode when the boys got out of hand. As they were just entering their teens, this came in handy. What I noticed and did not expect was that the firmer I learned to be, the softer Jim became. Where the scales of the balance had previously been tipped precariously to one side, they now were more aligned. It dawned on me one day that it was my fault Jim had to be so tough all those years. I had sent the message that I was unwilling to do my part, so Jim had to be firm for both of us. But as he saw me take on my responsibilities, he let go enough to make us equal partners in this important aspect of parenting.

As I became firmer in my discipline, I sent the message that I loved my sons enough to draw healthy boundaries for them. As I became fairer to my husband by shouldering my fair share of the disciplining, I sent the message that I cared enough about him to share the unpleasant tasks rather than dumping them all on him. I learned that just as Jesus loved His disciples, so I could also love my little disciples, and that included the ultimate act of love: discipline.

Discipline in love
Is love!

Do not despise the LORD's discipline
and do not resent his rebuke,
because the LORD disciplines those he loves,
as a father the son he delights in.

— PROVERBS 3:11–12

Lord,
My fear of losing love kept me from doing my fair share.
Thank You for teaching that when I discipline in love
     I send my children the message that they are loved
     I send my husband the message that he is loved
Thank You for showing me that discipline is
     Teaching
     Guiding
     Leading

In the same manner, Lord,
     Teach me
     Guide me
     Lead me
     Correct me
So that I can be the best mother I can be.

Amen.

Martha Stewart…
(No Matter How Hard I
Try to Be)…I Ain't!

I've been told that I physically resemble her, but that's where the similarities end, for I am anything but a domestic diva. Not for lack of trying! I pull out all the stops in my attempts to make the perfect piecrust or sew a straight seam. When *she* demonstrates her work it's always *perfect,* but my attempts usually resemble the truck stop version: my food tastes okay, but it tastes even better if you eat it with your eyes closed.

So, you can imagine how uncomfortable I felt when I went to my first Christmas cookie exchange. I don't know if all cookie exchanges are the same, but the one I went to was a bake-off of the most competitive kind. There was no prize, just pride to be won or lost at the end of the evening.

I arrived at the hostess's home, decorated as if it were the White House. The other young mothers arrived carrying plates of cookies that were true works of art. I, on the other hand, carried a plain plate piled high with peanut-butter-chocolate-chip cookies that I had thrown together at the last minute.

I really didn't want to go, but my husband thought it would

be good for me to mingle more with other mothers. So I had rushed to the store at the last minute to get the ingredients. I had barely managed to make dinner and change before I ran out the door, leaving dishes piled high in the sink.

There I stood in an immaculate home, carrying an intricately decorated cookie basket that someone else had made and handed to me when I walked through the door, filling it with a sampling of the amazing cookies along with copies of the recipes, artfully copied with stickers and special fonts. (I had scribbled mine, then xeroxed them at the grocery store.) The cookies that amazed me the most were the delightful mini gingerbread men. All outlined with a fine tip of white royal icing, with perfect bow ties, they looked too good to eat. It hardly seemed a fair exchange — those gingerbread men and other gourmet confections for my plain old chocolate-chip cookies.

I felt inadequate compared to the artful accomplishments all around me. My cookies were just one example. As I listened to the other young mothers describe how well their children were doing in school, in sports, and in music, I found myself again coming up short. They were all more beautiful, more talented, more disciplined — in essence, better mothers than I! They were the epitome of the perfect domestic diva. That night I learned — Martha Stewart I ain't!

Being forced to face my limitations was depressing and frustrating. As a woman whose dream it was to be an awesome mother, to discover I was lacking in this area — of all areas — was a rude wake-up call. I felt sorry for my poor deprived sons and husband.

Days later I looked inside the cookie bucket that contained the intricate confections I had collected at the cookie exchange.

The chocolate-chip cookies were gone that very night. The other cookies were for the most part left untouched, growing stale. I realized my boys didn't need artistic confections; they needed substantial food, fit for men. They could have cared less about how the cookies looked; they cared only about how they tasted. I realized through this experience that it was possible for me to be a good mother—even though Martha Stewart I ain't!

Indeed, it was a big mistake to try to compare myself with Martha, other mothers, even my own mother. God knew exactly what kind of mother my sons needed. *I am the best mother in the whole world for my sons!* My sons didn't need the gifts that all those other mothers had. They needed me—and only me! Conversely, I wouldn't have been a good mother for other children. Their mothers were perfect for them!

God created me perfectly just for my boys and their needs. And He knew exactly what gifts to give other mothers just for their children! God has a different plan for each of our lives—a wonderful, beautiful, *perfectly* created plan.

I am the perfectly created mother for my children.
You are the perfectly created mother for your children.
We are all part of God's perfectly created plan!

You created my inmost being;
you knit me together in my mother's womb.
I praise you because I am fearfully
and wonderfully made.

—Psalm 139:13–14

Lord,
Forgive me for comparing myself
       With Martha
       With other moms
       With my mother

Help me to see myself
       As the perfect mother
       For my children
       Gifted especially just for their needs

Protect me from looking around
Keep me focused on looking up
       To You,
              My God,
              My Creator,
       Who made me just the way
       I need to be—
       Perfectly gifted for my children!

Thank You, Lord!

             Amen.

Can a Working Mom
Be a Good Mom?

*T*he boys were busy playing in the backyard while I frantically worked at my computer in the kitchen, desperately trying to meet the deadline. I had been completely lost in my writing for hours. Every now and then I would glance out the window to make sure they were still alive and not covered with mud. It was nearly lunchtime when Jason came into the house looking for something to eat.

I brushed him aside. "In a minute. Let me finish this chapter. Go play with your brothers, and as soon as I'm done I'll make you some macaroni and cheese." I knew this was Jason's favorite dish. That year in kindergarten the teacher had assembled and made copies of a cookbook for Mother's Day. It was embarrassing as well as entertaining, as the cookbook comprised all the children's favorite recipes of foods prepared by their mothers. The children had dictated to their teacher what they could recall of their mother's recipes. There was one recipe for spaghetti that called for "hundreds of onions." Jason's favorite recipe of mine had been macaroni and cheese (I felt soo proud!). The instructions were simple. Even a kindergartner could follow them: "Open the box. Pour it into a pan. Cook for half of *Sesame Street*."

Promising macaroni and cheese to Jason was always a good ploy to buy me cooperation. But rather than go back outside and play as I had asked him, he noticed the bright red button on my old clunky word processor, and before I could stop him he reached over and pushed it. Just like that, the entire chapter I had written was completely gone!

"Oh, Jason! Look what you've done!" I cried. "Go back outside right now!"

I was beside myself. I was angry at Jason, though I knew I shouldn't be. How could I possibly meet my deadline now, with all these little boys underfoot needing to be fed and mothered? I had rationalized that they were fine playing outside, that they didn't need me, that I could get my work done and still be a good mother, but now half a day was gone, and I had nothing to show for it.

Another morning, years later, I was late for the office. I had an important meeting. People were flying in to meet with several of us on a project. It was imperative that I be there. I went to wake up the boys. Scott felt warm. "You okay, Scotty?" I asked anxiously. Truth be told, I was afraid he might be sick, and then how in the world was I going to be in two places at once?

"My stomach hurts." Just then he jumped out of bed and ran to the bathroom, barely making it to the toilet in time.

Great! The flu! There was no way he could go to school that day. I had to let people down — again.

I was a working mom. I have worked from home and I have worked in an office, and in both places, many times I have felt torn. I felt an obligation to my career, my deadlines, and my managers, not to mention my husband and my children. When I was a classroom teacher, it was even more difficult. I couldn't just call in sick. There were notes to be written for a substitute, and at times I had to bundle up a sick child in a blanket to ride with me to the school site, waiting in the car while I ran the notes into the school for that day. And there were limits to how many days off I could have without losing pay. If I lost pay, then we would have less income to pay for groceries that month.

I have worked for many reasons, financial as well as for a chance to follow my dreams, to build my career, and to have some adult companionship. Although working moms were very controversial at the time my boys were young, I had chosen to be one. I was aware that some people claimed it was better for children to be home with their mothers, yet I knew this was not something I could do without feeling resentment. I believed that a resentful mother would not be a good mother, so I worked outside the home as well as in the home.

But oh, did I feel guilty! The guilt was worst on those days when the dream of being a mother and the dream of having a career collided and crashed along with the chapter of a book or were derailed by sick child. There were many, many days when I beat myself up for neglecting my children by wanting to have a career. On those days I mentally chastised myself with an imaginary birch whip and the admonition, *Bad mom! Bad mom!*

But was I really? Did the boys really miss out by playing with one another all those mornings rather than playing with boring old Mom? Not if you ask them! The memories they cherish are not the same memories I cherish. They are grateful for the enriching activities I did with them, for it paid out in great dividends in their education, but they would not trade their times playing together for all the money in the world.

Did my children miss out because of my choice to work? Would they have turned out better if I had not pursued my career? Was I, in reality, a bad mom because they had to be in day care? Well, I couldn't be prouder of my sons than I am. They are accomplished and happy and we are very close as a family. As a school administrator I have seen many mothers who are called to the school from work to come pick up their sick children. The exasperated, worried, torn looks on their faces are very familiar to me. But I have also seen many, many children at our school who were raised by working mothers who grew up to be remarkable young adults.

My boys didn't miss out on anything. These other children didn't miss out on anything. If anybody missed out, it was all the mothers who chose to or had to work. How many more memories could I have had if I had spent more time with them? Every mother's choice or circumstance is different. It is impossible to define a plan that is best for all of God's children. No two of us are alike. In the final analysis it is between every mother and father and their children and God. Beyond that—it is nobody's business.

The secret to being content in whatever circumstance you find yourself is to trust God to fill in the gaps, follow behind, and clean up your mistakes; and to enjoy your children as much as possible. Put that whip away. Stop the "Bad Mom" self-flagellation. Raise your hand high in the air, turn your palm toward the wall behind you, reach back, and pat yourself on the back and say, "Good mom! Good mom!"

A working mom is a good mom
If she works at making sure she doesn't
Miss out on the memories!

I know what it is to be in need,
and I know what it is to have plenty.
I have learned the secret of being content
in any and every situation,
whether well fed or hungry,
whether living in plenty or in want.
I can do everything through him who gives me strength.

—Philippians 4:12–13

Jesus,
Grant me the ability to find that sweet balance
Of working for You as well as for my children
Keep me from losing out on precious time
Before it's lost for good
Remind me of the cost of lost memories
When I am tempted to think I can have it all

I have made some tough choices
Sometimes I chose wrong
At times I settled for less than Your best

Thank You for redeeming
    My choices
    My mistakes
    My follies

Help me to refrain from judging
>Others
>Myself
And in the process, lose even more than I already have
Keep me focused on all I have
Blessings too numerous to count
A life that is rich beyond measure
Because You saved me

>Amen.

Portrait of a *Real*-ly Good Mom

*T*here is a mother who stands out as a true supermom. I would like to introduce you to her. Perhaps the best way for you to get to know her is if I paint a verbal portrait of her. Let me begin by detailing what Supermom is *not*:

- She is *not* the most beautiful mother I know.
- She is *not* the most educated mother in the world.
- She is *not* the wealthiest mother around.
- She is *not* the wittiest mother I have ever known.
- She is *not* the best cook.

Let's take a look at a typical day in Supermom's life and see if you can discover what it is that makes her such an awesome mother.

The alarm goes off. "Is it morning already?" Unable to even open her eyes (yesterday was such a looong day), she hits the snooze button. "A few more minutes of sleep will be good for everybody," she rationalizes. Suddenly the light from the window casting a glow across her eyes awakens her in a panic.

Glancing at the clock, she realizes that she has overslept by more than a half hour!

Frantic, she tears through the house sounding the alarm. "It's late! Everybody up! Hurry! Now! Don't go back to sleep! You don't want to be late for school!"

She has jumped into the shower when she hears shouts of fighting coming from the room her two girls share. She throws on a robe without taking time to dry off and hollers down the hall, "Cut it out. I mean it!"

The fighting continues unabated as she dashes down to toss bowls, cereal, milk, and spoons on the table. She continues to hear harsh words and yells a little louder this time, "Stop it, now! If I have to come up there . . . !"

As she turns the coffeemaker on, she thinks, *Why am I not following up on my threat? And why am I doing everything for them?* Still, she yells, "Breakfast time!"

"Mom, she called me fat!"

"Did not."

"Did too!"

"Mom, she's wearing my new blouse. I told her to take it off!"

Supermom is at her wit's end. Her voice is getting louder and harsher as she says, "Just get down here, now! I mean it! You're going to be late for school and I'm going to be late for work!"

The Bible she had planned to read to them that morning gets buried under the dishtowels, and truth be told, she completely forgets about it thanks to oversleeping—again.

After several attempts to get the girls into the car, she screams, "If you don't get in the car now, I am going to leave without you and you can just walk to school!"

Pouting faces and stomping feet show the unhappy, resigned acceptance of their mother's threat. The girls suddenly push past each other in their efforts to get the front seat.

"It's my turn! She got the front seat yesterday."

"But I missed a turn on Monday when I was sick, so I'm owed another turn today."

"Move!"

The older sister pulls on the younger sister's arm, trying to pry her out of the front seat.

Supermom declares in her best Judge Judy voice to the sister pulling, "We'll make it up tomorrow. That's my final decision."

"But, Mom!"

"You girls are driving me crazy! Why can't you get along?"

Glancing a frantic look at herself in the mirror of the car while fidgeting with the radio, she pushes a loose strand of hair out of her eyes, takes a deep breath, and puts the car into reverse. Although this morning is not much different from most, the guilt begins to well up like persistent heartburn.

She looks at herself in the rearview mirror again. She doesn't like what she sees.

She breathes a prayer and realizes that perhaps there are more important aspects to being a mother than getting her kids to school on time. (I realize that every teacher who reads this is shuddering, but it's true!) Turning the car off, she turns to her girls and says, "I'm sorry. I shouldn't have yelled at you. I love both of you more than anything in the world. I try to get you to school on time because I think it's what I need to do to be a good mother."

Reaching into the glove compartment, she pulls out a

pocket Bible and reads a verse to her girls: "Whatever is true, whatever is noble, whatever is right, whatever is pure, whatever is lovely, whatever is admirable—if anything is excellent or praiseworthy—think about such things" (Phil. 4:8).

"Today, let's look for something true or pure or noble and share it at dinner. Thank you for loving me and forgiving me even when I lose my temper with both of you."

What is it about Supermom that makes her super? It's not because she has it all together, because she obviously doesn't. Just the opposite! She is a supermom because she is authentic, real, and brave enough to admit her failures and ask her children for forgiveness. She is a *real* mom and shares with her children that she is trying to be a good mother, which tells them she loves them.

The reality is that *any* mom who is a *real* mom is a supermom. A *real* mom teaches the most valuable lesson of all—how to admit mistakes and ask forgiveness.

A real-*ly good mother is simply*
A real *mother*
Who real-*ly loves God and her children!*

Each of you must put off falsehood
and speak truthfully to his neighbor,
for we are all members of one body.
"In your anger do not sin":
Do not let the sun go down while you are still angry.

— EPHESIANS 4:25–26

Dear Jesus, Savior and Friend,
Thank You for being a model of how to be
The mother You need me to be.

Give me the courage to be
     Real
     Authentic
Reveal to me when I am being
     Pretentious
     Fake

As I model to my children the ability to
     Admit when I've been wrong
     And repent when I've sinned
Against them and You
May they learn the freedom that can be theirs
As well as mine.

Amen.

Mommy Guilt = Good Mommy

For years I thought I was the only one who suffered from mommy guilt. And then I became a school administrator. Day after day, I saw mommies come through the office — not only mommies of the children who attended, but also mommies who worked in the office, and mommies who were teachers. As a result I have heard many, many confessions of mommy guilt over the years, and I suspect that, even so, what I've heard has gone through the filter of wanting to impress me.

* Last night I was up until three typing my daughter's paper. She had been asking me all week and I didn't have time for her. It was due today, and I already felt guilty for pushing her aside all week. If I were a better mother, I wouldn't have put her off until the last minute!

* My son was driving me crazy this morning. He was crying over every little thing. I lost my temper and told him to stop acting like a baby. I feel like a bad mom!

- I ran out of lunch food, so I had to stop at Taco Delight. What kind of mother feeds her kids this garbage? My conscience is really smarting!

- My son failed his spelling test this week. I was too tired to help him. I feel like the worst mother in the world!

- I can't get my three-year-old to go to bed before eleven. I have absolutely no control over him, and it's affecting my marriage. My husband and I have no time alone anymore. I'm beginning to resent my children. I feel terrible!

- I bought a new pair of shoes on sale for myself. I should have spent the money on my child. I am a selfish mother!

- I used the television as a babysitter instead of reading to my children so I could read my book. A good mother would have spent the time on them—not herself!

Other than mommy guilt, what do all these mommies have in common? Well, it may be hidden under the bad-mommy facade they are projecting, but they all love their children deeply. When I hear mommies talk like this, it verifies to me that these children are actually blessed children—they have mothers who care. Mommies who don't care don't feel the guilt. I worry about those kids whose mommies neglect their children without so much as a second thought.

Caring about your children comes with a price. You will find yourself losing sleep worrying about your child from time to time. You will find yourself on your knees, begging Christ for mercy, nearly every day. You will think things or even say things you will regret for the rest of your life. But you will also be an awesome mother! Caring comes with a price, but not caring comes with an even steeper price.

Mothers who don't care — how can that be, you ask? For all of us mommies who beat ourselves up daily with mommy guilt, such an attitude is unfathomable. The fact that you feel mommy guilt (and that fact has already been established, dear reader, or why else would you be reading this book?) is evidence that you care. The fact that you care — in the final analysis — is what counts the most! A caring mother is a good mother!

The fact that you feel mommy guilt means you are a wonderful mother! It also means you will carry your cares with you, and you run the risk of being burdened by them unless you learn to cast your cares at the foot of the cross.

Good mothers → caring → carrying cares → guilt
Stop carrying the cares!
Drop them! At the foot of the cross!

Cast all your anxiety on him because he cares for you.

— 1 PETER 5:7

Gracious God,
Thank You for caring about me so much
That You sent Your Son to die for me
As a result I can cast my cares
At Your feet!

Grant me the courage to keep caring
Even though it will cost me, in terms of
     Sleep
     Peace of mind
     Guilt

Grant me the ability to share the burden
To allow You to help me carry
     My cares

Free me from the tyranny of thinking that
     I have to do
          All of this
          All by myself

With You by my side, shouldering my cares for me,
I will dare to care deeply about my children
For in the final analysis, they are ultimately
      Your children!

        Amen.

Being Care-ful About What
You Care About

*A*s a mother she made me shudder. I have seen mothers of all types, but she was the first to make me cringe.

I could overhear her in a restaurant—I confess to eavesdropping. The conversation was just too intriguing to resist. Besides, she was talking very loudly, apparently not caring that everyone around could hear her.

To make matters worse, she was old enough to know better. Her children were not children anymore; they were young adults. She was complaining that her house (which she claimed was over four thousand square feet) was too small. As a result she was demanding that her husband buy her a larger house. No attempt was made to hide her cleavage, which was likely paid for, along with puffed lips, as she and her friend had just finished comparing notes on their plastic surgeons. But what alarmed me the most was the story of her recent trip to a club to drink with her daughter to celebrate her twenty-first birthday, where she even went so far as to pick up a man for her daughter. (I'm not making this up—I wish I were!)

I admit to being totally judgmental where she was concerned. I confess I judged her values because they were anti-thetical to mine. What she cared about, I do not care about. In fact, her priorities scared me. I had overheard a mother who was sending her children the message that superficial appear-ances (both physical and material) were of utmost importance. She was teaching her children that their value lay in how they look, what they possessed, and how popular they were. The problem is that her children will grow up caring about the same things she cares about.

There is another mother I know who is one of the best I have met. She works tirelessly to help the homeless. She herself was homeless at one point in her life. She found Jesus at a local church, and, through the church members' help, she managed to get herself back on her feet. If you met her today, you would never guess that she had once made her bed out on the street. She is a lovely, young, professional mother. Married, with chil-dren and a new life, she has dedicated herself to teaching her children about serving others. She is a leader who organizes food drives, coat drives, shoe drives, and soup kitchens within her community. Her children can be found at her side, helping out those less fortunate. In fact, Je'net and her husband recently started a nonprofit ministry and opened a seventeen-bed shel-ter for women and children in desperate need.

Je'net is sending her children the message that they can make a difference in their world. They are learning the joy that comes from helping others. They care not about the size of their home, their material acquisitions, or their popularity. They care about those who need help.

I learned from both of these mothers that it is extremely important to be careful about what it is you care about, for whatever you care about—so will your children. If you care about appearance, your children will care about appearance. If you care about material acquisitions, your children will care about material success. If you care about helping others, your children will care about making a difference. If you care about spiritual matters, your children will care about spiritual growth.

I have a friend whose children always cleaned their rooms. I could never get mine to do it, so I always did it for them. My friend and I are two mothers who have two completely disparate approaches to mothering—but our children today, as young adults, are more alike than you might imagine. Our children are friends, so I have even been privy to seeing their dorm rooms. There's not much difference between the rooms of my friend's kids and my boys'. In fact, it amazes me how neat my sons have become as they have matured. I always worried that I was making a mistake by cleaning up for them, but I just couldn't seem to help myself.

How do you explain this phenomenon? How do children raised so completely differently turn out so much alike? Well, even though our methodology was totally different (I still think her method was better), our children picked up on what it was we cared about. Both Michelle and I care about keeping a neat house. Both of us care about spiritual matters. Our children are all very involved in church and pursuing spiritual endeavors.

What you care about—what you value—will always supersede how you raise your children. It's not as important *how* you raise your children. It is, however, of paramount importance *what* you care about. I wasted many hours of worrying needlessly that I wasn't doing everything the right way. In reality, that which I cared most about was being transmitted unwittingly to my children. Like the air they breathed, it was part of their environment.

So, try to relax. And don't worry so much about your methodology. If you must worry about something (and I am one of those), worry about what you value and how you communicate that to your children. The truth is this: you can never fool a child—especially your own. Without even realizing it, they will adopt your passions (don't confuse interests with values) and your concerns. If you care about it—so will they! So, it is important to carefully care about what you care about!

Carefully care about what you *care about!*
Then relax and enjoy your children!

Train a child in the way he should go,
and when he is old he will not turn from it.

— PROVERBS 22:6

Lord and Savior,
I thought I messed up in how I taught my kids
But today I see that I did fine

I taught them about You
I taught them how to pray
I taught them how to believe
    In You
    In others
    In themselves

Thank You for forgiving me, redeeming me, and drawing
    me ever closer to You
The closer I am to You, the more my children will seek to
    be close to You.

What a gift! I can never thank You enough!

Amen.

Listening with Your Ears, Eyes, Heart!

*I*t had been a long day, but there was still this pile of dirty pots and pans to finish washing, clothes from the dryer that had yet to be folded, and lunches to be made. Homework was still waiting and Jason had a book report that had to be typed. My hands were deep in the sink of dishes and warm soap suds. Scott, seven years old, tugged on my sleeve. "Mom, today at school, Brandon . . ."

Suddenly he stopped talking to me.

I scrubbed hard at the baked-on enchilada sauce. "Go ahead, Scott."

"No."

The spot was stubborn and my wrist was beginning to get sore. I reached under the sink to get the cleanser. "Go ahead, I'm listening."

"No, you're not!"

"Of course I am. You said, 'Today at school, Brandon,' and then you stopped talking to me."

"I need you to listen, Mom."

Ah, there was the cleanser! At first I couldn't find it behind the window cleaner, the furniture polish, and the dishwasher soap, but there it was, a little rusty, a tad crusty, but cleanser doesn't have an expiration date, right? Now, where was that wool pad I rarely needed? I continued to dig around under the sink.

"I need you to listen to me, Mom." This was now addressed to my denim-clad rear end.

"I told you, Scott. I can hear you."

"Mom," he said with exasperation, "I need you to listen with your eyes!"

Oh, my! I had been listening with my ears, but not my heart. Scott had been trying to tell me that I was only half listening. I thought I could juggle listening with doing the laundry, the dishes, and the other endless tasks. This had been the hallmark of my mothering—multitasking—and I was proud of it. The more tasks I could accomplish simultaneously, the more efficient I felt.

The Mother's Day gift that Christopher had given me said it all. "Supermom" was etched along the bottom of a figurine of a mother with a tool belt strapped around her waist, a phone in one hand, a spoon in another, and babies clinging to one leg and another strapped on her back. The figurine was too close for comfort. I prided myself on the fact that I could listen to my children while vacuuming the family room and carrying a baby on my back.

But Scott's words stopped me cold. I tried to think of one time when I had listened to my sons with my eyes—when I had given them my full attention. Most of the time they talked to my back or the side of my face as I folded clothes, made beds, packed lunches, or cooked dinner.

I dried my hands and turned my back, this time not on my child — but on my tasks. I sat down at the kitchen table and said, "You're right, Scott. I need to listen with my eyes."

I looked in my dear son's eyes — dark hazel eyes, striking with his white-blond hair. How much time had I lost — not looking my sons in the face? How much of their souls had I missed seeing because I had focused my attention on my list of things to do?

I learned a valuable lesson that day: to write a different list from there on out. To include — indeed, put number one on the list — looking into the eyes of God, and looking into the eyes of my sons and my husband — every day. Although I am humbled to admit that I didn't change that much — I still said yes to too many projects — I wonder how much more I would have lost out on if Scott had not forced me to see what I had been missing.

The key to capturing your child's soul is to:
Listen with your eyes.
Hear with your heart.

There is nothing hidden that will not be disclosed,
and nothing concealed that will not be known
or brought out into the open.
Therefore consider carefully how you listen.

—LUKE 8:17–18

Lord,
I got my priorities all jumbled again.
I let the calendar drive my agenda
Instead of my child's needs.

Thank You for opening my eyes
For letting me see
> My child's needs . . .
> My oversights . . .
> Before it was too late!

Keep me focused, Lord,
On what's most important.
> Not an impeccable house
> Not a completely-crossed-off list
But the souls of my children

Help me to see what You see
> When You look in their eyes.
Help me to see how much You love me
> When I look into *Your* eyes.

Amen.

Battles Worth Fighting — and Those That Aren't

*I*t was Wednesday night. I only had that night and the next to get Christopher ready for his spelling test. Christopher struggled in school. More than once after a parent-teacher conference I ducked into the nearest ladies' room, closed the door of the stall, and silently wept. The teacher always suggested getting him tested, but I resisted on the grounds that I didn't want him labeled. In years to come, this was a decision I questioned.

Spelling tests were something I could help with and feel some semblance of pride and hope for Christopher's academic success. As a result, the grades for his spelling tests were passing, but it was taking a toll on our relationship. The battles after dinner were draining for both of us. Like a mother possessed, I rifled through his backpack every Monday to find his spelling list. I immediately posted it on the fridge door. I would drill him verbally on the way to school, and when I picked him up on Fridays from school the first words out of my mouth were "How did you do on your spelling test?"

Christopher's struggles in school eventually drew me into a midlife career change. At the age of forty, I found myself earning a teaching credential as well as a master's in curriculum and instruction. All of the courses I was taking included assignments, which were frequently papers I had to write. The topics were usually ours to choose, but the process always required our exploring what we could find in published research articles. Every paper I wrote for my program focused on areas of learning that were difficult for Christopher. The real blessing for me, however, was that as a student in such a program, I had the opportunity to build relationships with professors I consulted for years to come regarding my son's challenges.

One night, I was proudly relaying a new strategy I had devised to help Christopher with his spelling. I expected my professor to be impressed, but instead she quietly asked, "How important is spelling—I mean, what with spell-check and all? Perhaps writing for meaning is more important, yes?"

She had this way of getting me to stop and really think. And I did a lot of thinking about what she said! Then I did something that took a lot of courage for me. I took a deep breath, then held my breath, and—didn't help Christopher with his spelling. Boy, was that hard to do! I somehow refrained from asking him anything about it for the entire week. I didn't dig the list out of his backpack. We didn't sit down after dinner and battle our way through his spelling list.

On Friday, I bit my lip to keep from blurting out, "How did you do on your test?"

I was sure he had failed it. I had no doubt I had completely neglected my mommy duties and that I had just earned the award for Worst Mommy of the Week. Without my weekly feedback—without *my* passing grade in spelling—I feared that I had failed as a mother by allowing my son to fail without trying to rescue him.

Somehow I managed to wait until Chris was outside playing with his brothers to check his backpack. Sure enough — there was the test. His grade had dropped a little — but not much at all. I was stunned! I had been putting my poor little boy through spelling boot camp every week, and it hadn't made that much difference. It suddenly dawned on me that I had been doing it for me as much as for my son.

I never helped him with another spelling test. I still checked his grades to make sure that he wasn't failing, but I never asked him about them again. Then, I began to read to him. My husband and I (based on what my professor recommended) decided to read aloud to our sons throughout elementary school. Eventually my husband became the primary reader because I usually fell asleep. The boys got tired of poking me awake at every other sentence. As a result, my sons grew up cuddled around their father on the couch or in bed hearing him read The Chronicles of Narnia and other wonderful examples of children's literature.

What was more important: spelling or learning the love of language? Fortunately for my sons, I had wise counsel and it made all the difference in the world. Christopher still is not the best speller in the world, but you should read the papers he writes today in seminary! (Or you could try to! As for me, I can't decipher the Greek exegesis.)

I shudder to think how close I came to wasting even more time on such inconsequentials as spelling tests. How much enjoyment would my sons have missed out on if it hadn't been for a wise mentor? Their childhoods have come and gone. I have only memories now. But our memories are that much sweeter because we were liberated from getting stuck in artificial measurements and superficial gauges of how we were doing as parents.

As an administrator I have heard many moms' strategies for helping their children with spelling. I have a hard time not smiling. (The last thing I want them to think is that I am laughing at them or not taking them seriously.) Over the years I continue to be utterly amazed at how pervasive the need is for us moms to prove ourselves through spelling tests.

As a parent, and as an administrator, I have often asked myself, *Is this a battle worth fighting?* After raising four sons who fought all the time, the fewer battles I had to tackle, the better. Why waste energy on taking on challenges that, in the end, are silly? Why not focus my energies on what really matters?

After all, there is really so little time. I have regretted the time I spent fighting battles that were silly. I have never regretted playing with my children and reading to them. I have never regretted pushing them to do and be the men I thought they should be. I have never regretted watching them thrive in following God's plan for their lives.

Regrets? Yes! But only in fighting battles that Weren't worth it!

A wife of noble character who can find?
She is worth far more than rubies. . . .
She is clothed with strength and dignity;
she can laugh at the days to come.
She speaks with wisdom,
and faithful instruction is on her tongue. . . .
Her children arise and call her blessed;
her husband also, and he praises her:
"Many women do noble things, but you surpass them all."

—Proverbs 31:10, 25–26, 28–29

Lord,
I have so many regrets:
I lost

Precious moments
Priceless memories
Because I majored in the minors

How often didn't I fight a battle that was
Already lost?
I should have walked away
Or thrown in the towel
But pride . . .
Stupid,
Vain,
Foolish Pride

Propelled me to dig my heels in and make a fuss
Resulting in tears, anger, rebellion

How often did I turn my back on the battle that was
        Worth dying for?
I should have had more courage
        And dared to take a stand
But fear . . .
        Paralyzing
        Debilitating
        Unfounded fear
Held me back from fighting for what was right
Resulting in failure to help where they needed help the
        most

Help me, Lord, to discern
Which battles are already lost
Which battles are worth dying for.

Thank You, Jesus!
        For fighting for me
        For dying for me
        For living for me!

                Amen.

Brothers: Sibling Rivals?
Or Friends for Life?

*M*y futile attempt to prevent sibling rivalry started the moment I birthed Chris, our second boy in just two years' time. Jason had so fulfilled our lives that I had no desire to have another child. His smiles, his playful antics, his insatiable curiosity (every toy was immediately turned over and examined from the bottom as well as the top) provided endless delight. He was the center of our universe from first thing in the morning to that last prayerful cuddle as I tucked him in bed at night.

Then, when Jason was just a little over a year old, my period was late — and I was never late. With each passing day, I began to think that maybe, contrary to my carefully laid plans, I was pregnant again. My emotions quickly transformed from nervous fear to tender love for an unborn child that I might be carrying. Seven days later, however, when I started to spot, I realized that I wasn't pregnant, and the sorrow, the grief for a life that had never been took my heart by surprise. So, Jim and I decided to have another baby. Chris was conceived that month.

When Chris was born, Jim made valiant attempts to keep

Jason from feeling left out—pushed out—of our attention and affection. First he smuggled Jason into the hospital to see Mommy and the new baby "brudder" (back then children under twelve were not allowed, not even siblings). He also gave Jason a present—a Hungry, Hungry Hippos game (which he played with Jason for hours on end)—the day we brought Chris home from the hospital. In the days and months to come, we made sure we both continued to lavish attention on Jason for fear he would feel displaced.

Although Jason was an active baby, demanding endless attention, he was easy to care for. Whenever I put him down to sleep, he would smile up at me, close his eyes, and go promptly to sleep. I smugly watched other mothers struggle with their babies. I was arrogantly convinced that Jason's behavior was a result of our exemplary parenting.

Then Chris was born. Everything that worked for Jason backfired when it came to Chris. Chris refused to be put down once he had fallen asleep nursing or sipping on a bottle. But, during the day, where Jason required endless attention, Chris was content to lie happily for hours on a blanket or in his baby chair, breaking into a broad grin whenever someone took a moment to notice him. Jason and Chris couldn't have been more different. I learned from the moment Chris was born that my parenting had far less influence (if any at all) than I had once thought. This epiphany vacillated as good news or bad news, depending on whether I was feeling like a good mother or a bad one.

Surprisingly, when Chris was born, Jason didn't exhibit any signs of the sibling rivalry Jim and I had anticipated. However, Scott was born a mere twelve months later. My husband was chortling over friends of ours who had just learned they were unexpectedly expecting another child: "Don't they know how to prevent these things? We live in a modern age, after all."

I gave him a tight, wan smile. I hadn't told him I was late. *Be careful what you accuse others of, for eating crow is a bitter meal,* I thought.

It was just a week later that I called Jim and asked if we could meet for lunch. As we were ushered to our booth in the restaurant, he looked puzzled at the wrapped box I carried under my arm. "What is it, Sheila? It's not my birthday."

"You have to wait."

"It's not our anniversary."

"You'll see."

His curiosity was deepened when he opened and read the card: "The first test said, 'No.' The second test said, 'Yes.' God's ideas are always best."

"What does that mean?"

"Open the present."

Then he opened the box. Inside were two baby booties.

"Oh? *Oh! Really?*"

With tears shimmering in my eyes, I nodded. "Yes. We're having another baby."

"Oh, Sheila! I couldn't be happier! This is the best present you could have given me!"

Of course Chris, at ten months, was far too young to be affected by my impending third birth. But how would Jason fare, having just made room for first one sibling and now another so soon? Jason was astute well beyond his nearly three years of age. Just weeks before my due date, he looked at Jim with baby Chris in his arms, and then up at me, holding Jason's little hand, and back to my belly. He said, "Two kids, two parents. Who's going to take care of the new baby?"

So who knows what his motive was when he chose to bury Scott? Scott was just a day or two old when I heard a muffled cry from the nursery. The sound, which was so obviously abnormal, alarmed me. Racing to his side, I saw, much to my horror, no baby in the crib—just a heap of blankets mewing like a kitten. Big brother Jason had taken *every* blanket from Scott's closet and placed them (lovingly?) on his baby brother.

Although motive was never determined, it didn't really matter. I knew that I could not let this baby out of my sight again. Locks were installed on doors; baby gates went up to keep big brothers out of the kitchen while I cooked with the baby on the inside and brothers on the outside. Talk about creating a have/have not situation, which is always a fertile breeding ground for sibling rivalry! Somehow my sons and I physically and emotionally survived those early years, though there were many close calls.

As typical boys, they were very physical. They acted like puppies or bear cubs, tumbling, nipping, wrestling whenever and wherever they could—the grocery store, the doctor's office, Grandpa and Grandma's living room. Their favorite form of entertainment was to roughhouse with one another. And as any mother of boys knows, roughhousing is an inevitable train wreck waiting to happen and always led to tears. Consequently I spent most of my energy trying to *avoid* conflict ("Stop, before someone gets hurt!") or trying to *resolve* conflict ("All of you—on time-out—now!").

I was convinced that it was my job to prevent sibling rivalry and I was obviously failing miserably! Of course, that just gave me one more thing to feel guilty about! So, I devoured books on sibling rivalry. Nothing worked.

One "expert" recommended giving every child his or her own date night. The reasoning: that way they would know that even if I couldn't give them my full concentration right then, they could look forward to having uninterrupted time with me on their specified nights.

I can't believe I even bothered reading this. First of all, this "expert" had only one child, so what could she know about sibling rivalry? Second, what preschool-age child is mature enough to understand delayed gratification and to willingly wait a minute, much less days, to have their needs met? Third, who has enough nights in the week for *five* date nights (four kids and a husband)?

It wasn't until years later, on the job, that I learned avoiding sibling rivalry was not only futile, it was also not always desirable. As a full-time school administrator I found, much to my dismay, that 90 percent of my job consisted of conflict resolution. As a person who innately seeks harmony, I approached my job the same way I dealt with my boys and their fighting: trying at all costs to avoid conflict and keep the peace. It was in my doctoral program (just a few years ago) that I learned conflict is not always a bad thing. Conflict can be healthy. (Heaven forbid! This was not news I wanted to hear!) It can keep us from going the wrong way and getting hurt. It can challenge us to be the best we can be. It does not always need to be avoided, but it does always need to be resolved in a timely, healing way or it can turn into bitterness.

Although it seemed that our house was the scene of non-stop fighting, somehow, in spite of my futile attempts to be a peacemaker, they emerged as friends. Today I suspect that all that roughhousing, all that "conflict," was God's means of brotherly bonding.

Two years ago at Christmas, Jason gave his brothers a gift that made this old mommy's heart sing. He gathered his three brothers and gave each of them (and himself as well) a gift — a solid, thick, silver "brother's" ring — with this introduction: "Wear this to remember we are brothers through thick and thin. We are not only brothers. We are friends — forever!"

I merely birthed four brothers.
All I had to do was truly love them all equally,
And keep them from killing one another long enough
For God to forge them into friends — for life!

The wisdom that comes from heaven
is first of all pure; then peace-loving, considerate,
submissive, full of mercy and good fruit,
impartial and sincere.
Peacemakers who sow in peace raise a harvest of righteousness.

—JAMES 3:17–18

As iron sharpens iron,
so one man sharpens another.

—PROVERBS 27:17

Prince of Peace,
These children of yours,
Are equally
      Created
      Loved
      Valued.

They are birthed into one home
May it be . . .
      A home of fun
      A home of laughter
      A home of love

When conflicts arise over
     Things
     Time
     Attention
     Affection

Help me to teach my children that
     Sometimes equal isn't fair
     Sometimes going without is gain
     Sometimes giving is getting
Thank You for being the ultimate Peacemaker
Demonstrating with Your life that
Peace comes only with sacrifice.

May the children learn that
No matter how fiercely conflicted
Their lives may become,
     They can live in true peace
     When they live in *Your* peace.

Amen.

Past Shames: "Can I Spare My Daughter the Same?"

She sat across from me, her eyes filled with tears, and her voice broke.*

When we first met she had told me her story about how she had been redeemed in her early twenties from a wild youth. She had been enmeshed in a world of drugs and sexcapades, when one day she hit bottom. One morning she looked at her disheveled appearance in the mirror and, much like a prodigal daughter, had returned home broken, ashamed, and afraid to look anyone in the eyes.

Her mother, who had prayed for her every night, kneeling by her bed, wrapped her daughter in her arms when she came limping home. That Sunday after church, the young woman waited around and talked to the pastor after the service and gave her life to Christ. She left church as a reborn, new woman, forgiven and redeemed.

It wasn't long before she met a wonderful young Christian man who fell in love with her. He knew about her past, but he

*This woman is a compilation of several mothers I have met with this issue. My responses are, in essence, what I told each of them.

saw only a redeemed, beautiful Christian woman. They married, and a few years later she bore a beautiful baby girl. That daughter was now approaching adolescence, and my friend was besieged by anxiety.

"Sheila, you know what my life was like before I met Christ. I know I've been forgiven and redeemed for my previous lifestyle, but now that my daughter is getting older, I'm finding myself so afraid!"

Her tears suddenly burst and as they rolled down her cheeks, she put her hands over her face and gave in to the grief and fear and sobbed uncontrollably.

"What are you afraid of?"

"I am afraid that she will be ashamed of me, but more than that I am afraid . . ."

"Take your time."

Christine took a big breath and wiped her eyes. "I am afraid that . . . that . . . she will make the same mistakes I made. I would do anything to spare her that hurt! Even though I know I am a new creation in Christ, I cannot forgive myself. The shame of being with other men still haunts me, especially now that I am the mother of a beautiful daughter."

My heart broke for this young mother whose life was gradually being eroded by the corrosion of unresolved guilt. Shame was not only stealing her joy, it was also filling her life with fear.

"What is purity?" I asked her.

"It is saving yourself for marriage."

"What is impurity?"

"It is allowing yourself to be intimate with someone before it is safe."

"Well," I gently guided, "I suppose you could use those definitions. But let's look at diamonds for a minute. All diamonds contain trace elements that are impure. The purer the diamond, the more it is worth. But the jeweler's task is to cut the stone so as to create a gem that has the fewest impurities possible. But it is not possible to be completely pure. In reality, I don't believe that true purity actually exists."

"But——"

"Hang in there with me. Sure, it is preferable to enter marriage without the baggage of memories and hurts that comes with being intimate prior to being wed. But the Bible tells us that we all have sinned. Scripture does not say that one sin is worse than another. Why are you beating yourself up for your mistake, when *all* of us have made mistakes?"

"I am just so ashamed!"

"But if you never felt ashamed, would you ever have felt the grace?"

"No."

"Let's go back to the diamond analogy. Jesus died on the cross for your shame, so you don't have to carry that anymore—— unless you choose to. You can lay that burden down. When we allow Jesus to be the Master Jeweler and carve the impurities out of our lives, He shapes us into brilliant gems—— mothers who know how much it hurts to be used, mothers who can teach their daughters, mothers who can understand when they need to, as well as mothers who can pray for God's protection. You can be a mother who gives her daughter the message that sexual purity can save a world of hurt—— yet if she crosses a line that results in her feeling shamed, you can show her how to find freedom from it."

She is not the only mother who has confided such fears to me, and in my experience this is mommy guilt at its most insidious. Mothers who were sexually active in their youth regret their actions because of the shame that inevitably results. And now that they are mothers, they would give anything to erase the guilt, if not the past, and do anything to prevent their daughters from similar fates.

Shame keeps us from looking into the face of God. Yet that is the very place we need to look. In *The Lion, the Witch and the Wardrobe,* Edmund was ashamed to look into Aslan's face. Aslan, the great lion, represents Jesus in the classic tales by C. S. Lewis. Edmund was guilty. Expecting to see anger, fearing he would see disappointment, he kept his gaze on the ground. When eventually he found the courage to look up into Aslan's face, he was stunned to see loving, caring, golden lion tears.

Looking into the face of God erases our shame and even restores our pride. Forgiveness redeems us. We find atonement. Now, having walked the walk, we can show our children the way. We can encourage them to look into the face of God and find love and forgiveness.

Freedom from shame, freedom from fear,
Freedom to love and be loved:
It comes from looking into the face of God!

You will lift up your face without shame;
you will stand firm and without fear.

—Job 11:15

Lord and Savior,
Shame

      For what I have said . . .
      For what I have done . . .
Haunts me

Only You can carve out the impurities in me
Only You can take the rough stone that is me
And cut and polish until I shine and glisten—
      A diamond—a priceless gem!

Help me to make peace with my past
So I can face my child's future with
      Faith
      Instead of fear.

Instead of turning my back to You
I turn my face to You
And look into Your eyes to see . . .
      Love!
      Redemption!
      Salvation!

Thank You, Lord!

           Amen.

Indulging in Some
Not-So-Guilty Pleasures!

*A*hh, this was the moment I looked forward to all day long. After being buried in messy diapers, piles of laundry, dirty dishes, deadlines, tackling traffic, making dinner, and cleaning up the kitchen, I always ended my day by soaking in a hot bubble bath with a chocolate treat (either a cup of hot cocoa or two or three dark Hershey's Kisses) and a good book.

Oh, the indulgence of a fragrant, steaming bubble bath, the glow of candles, and rich chocolate melting in my mouth— what an inexpensive, well-deserved treat this was! And I indulged on a daily basis. Not too surprisingly, the warm bubbles would have barely caressed my shoulders, I would have savored one sip of cocoa when, in a matter of minutes, I would fall asleep. How many books did I fish out of the tub?

So why bother? Even though I knew I would fall asleep, and the treat would last only a few minutes, it was *time for myself*. No one ever bothered me when I was in my bubble bath, except my husband, who always worried that I'd accidentally drown: "Wake up, Sheila, and go to bed."

For me, this was the best way to end my day even if it was for such a fleeting moment. And I knew I could look forward to it the next night and the next night and the next!

Did I feel guilty for indulging in such a daily luxury? Not on your life! Did I ever feel it was a waste of water for two minutes of bliss? Never! Did I ever regret allowing myself the fat and sugar of the chocolate? Not once! I deserved it. I earned those moments. I had given of myself selflessly all day long, and to treat myself at the end of the day kept me from being resentful or feeling cheated. I was worth it! After all, I was a child of God—His precious daughter. And taking care of myself—indulging myself—was a way of caring for one of God's children—in this case, me!

Knowing I had this to look forward to at the end of the day helped me be a more patient mother when all heck broke loose (as it seemed to do every day). There were times I would actually close my eyes for a second and imagine lowering myself into the soothing bubble bath. Although fleeting, this anticipation helped keep me from losing my temper more than once.

I actually tried it during the day one time. "That's it!" I yelled. "All of you—you are on time-out in your bedrooms. I am going to take a bath—and no one is going to disturb me!"

With supper in the oven, I was sure I could steal a moment to carry me through the rest of the hurdles that still lay ahead of me that day. As I drew my bubble bath I wondered why I hadn't thought of this before! But I was no sooner in the tub than I heard the sounds of boisterous fighting erupting from the boys' bedrooms. Then I heard the garage door open and Jim's footsteps in the hall running to the boys' rooms. I could hear Jim talking firmly to the boys and then he burst into our room.

"Sheila, do you know what they were doing?"

"N-n-no."

"When I drove into the driveway I could see them out on the roof! They had climbed out of their windows and were crawling on their hands and knees from one dormer to the next. And in their underwear, no less!"

I leaped out of the tub, threw my jeans back on, and raced to their bedrooms just in time to see Jim pounding five-inch nails into the window. They stayed nailed shut until the day we sold the house and moved out, nearly twenty years later, when he finally removed the nails.

Needless to say—that was the last time I tried a midday escape!

Finding a time and a place that work is no easy feat. It takes some thinking and planning, and it is all too easy to neglect finding a moment's escape and in the process neglect ourselves. But moms who take the time to take care of themselves are better moms. Love your child as you love yourself!

Love all God's children—especially you!
For you are—first and foremost—God's child!

Jesus replied: "'Love the Lord your God with all your heart
and with all your soul and with all your mind.'
This is the first and greatest commandment.
And the second is like it: 'Love your neighbor as yourself.'"

— MATTHEW 22:37–39

Heavenly Father,
Thank You for the countless blessings
The endless treats
The not-so-guilty pleasures
        That are Your gift to me!

Open my eyes
And my heart
        To see
        And receive
Help me not to take these
Gifts from a generous father
        For granted — or worse —
        To reject them
        To not accept them
For fear of not deserving them

Help me understand that You
        Long to bless me,
        As much as I long to bless my children

Protect me from the temptation
        To give in to being a martyr
        By denying myself
        Of Your gifts

Thank You, Lord,
For Your patience
And Your generous love.

                    Amen!

Be Fair to Yourself—Avoid Unfair Comparisons!

I have a love-hate relationship with the magazines that scream at me in the grocery checkout line. I love to read the headlines, the promises of an easy fix, whether it be for dinner, weight loss, or fashion. But the models who adorn the covers are enough to make any mom gag, especially if she is still nursing and her children are making a fuss. Seeing the glamorous images of impossibly thin waistlines and perky breasts caressed by plunging necklines, the epitome of sex goddesses, while one of my toddlers rubs his runny nose in my soft, round tummy, does absolutely nothing to fuel hot romantic evenings with my husband.

But it was the cover of a magazine featuring a well-known television personality that got to me the most. Everyone knew she was a young mother. She appeared every evening on television, looking like a model, and here she was on the cover of a household magazine, looking fresh, skinny, and beautiful. It was the headline that fatally stabbed my self-esteem, stomping my pitifully limited supply of self-confidence into oblivion, leaving me feeling totally deflated and defeated. Splashed across the glossy magazine was the million-dollar question, "How does she do it all?"

How does *she do it all?* I wondered. How *does* she manage to have a successful career, look like a model, raise beautiful children, have a happy marriage, and who knows what all else? Hoping to find another easy fix, I bought the magazine.

I looked at my image in the car mirror as I got ready to back out of the store parking place. My mousy, stringy hair was pulled into a ponytail; my lipstick had disappeared hours ago; and my drab, ordinary image paled compared to those I had just had thrust into my face while sorting through coupons and pulling begging, wrestling boys away from the candy.

It wasn't until hours later that I found time to read the article, eager to learn a secret that would make over my less-than-glamorous existence as a mommy. I imagined myself picking up some ingenious tips that would revolutionize my appearance and my time management. Her photos inside were just as impressive as the cover—even more so, because her children were also included in these photos and they looked amazing! Their clothes, their shoes, their haircuts were immaculate.

As I read the article I found myself torn between feelings of relief, disappointment, and outright anger. It turned out that she didn't do it all—after all! She did it with the help of a team of full-time nannies, assistants, a stylist (who picked out her clothes for her), a hairdresser (every day!), a makeup artist, a personal trainer, a housekeeper, and a cook. No wonder!

I was disappointed because I hadn't learned anything *I* could use. However, I was also vastly relieved because, in truth, her *entourage* was doing it all. And in subsequent tabloid headlines, it was announced that the photos had been significantly touched up* and her marriage had sadly (especially for the children) ended in divorce.

Although I did not learn the secrets I had hoped for, I did learn the secret God wanted me to learn: to start being fair to myself. I had been making unfair comparisons between others and myself. In the process I was doing a serious disservice to my children, my husband, and most of all—myself.

I do not begrudge this woman's fiscal ability to hire such assistance. However, I do resent the misleading photos and headlines, and the insinuation that we too could do it all when in fact none of us could do it all by ourselves—at least not as well! I also rebuked myself for falling for the lies, especially the trap of unfair comparisons—indeed, comparisons of any kind!

I am uniquely me—made exactly the way God wanted me to be. I can always learn how to make the most of who I am. It is my responsibility to develop the gifts God gave me and use them for His glory, but it is never a good idea to compare. That's where lies and insecurities can threaten my confidence and steal my joy. It's my responsibility to refrain from unfair comparisons and celebrate my uniqueness—as hard as that may be!

*Being fair to myself includes
Refraining from unfair comparisons!*

---

* In the interest of fair play, please be aware that I am likewise guilty of having my photo retouched for this book. In fact I vainly requested the photographer to please Photoshop out all my wrinkles, age spots, and triple chins. As a result, when my boys saw it they said, "Mom, you look twenty years younger!"

One thing I do:
Forgetting what is behind
and straining toward what is ahead,
I press on toward the goal to win the prize
for which God has called me heavenward in Christ Jesus.

— PHILIPPIANS 3:13–14

Lord, Father, my Creator,
Help me to be gracious
Not just to others — but also to myself.

Help me to be faithful
To not only my family
And my Creator
But also to Your creation
Me!

Guard my thoughts
Protect me from
Judging myself by
        How I look
        How I act
        How I love

Based on man's standards
Versus Yours
Thank You for creating me to be
The mother You — and my children —
Need me to be!

Amen.

No Time to Pray—What's a Christian Mother to Do?

When I was a youth pastor, I had the luxury of starting my mornings steeped in God's Word and prayer and communion with my Lord and Savior. That was when I was young and single. I had heard the message (and taught the same message to the youth I worked with) that daily devotions were essential to being a good Christian. So, it was a reasonable, logical conclusion that daily devotions were essential to my being a good Christian mother.

So, I purposely got up early before the boys awoke so I could spend time with God before the day erupted. It was five thirty in the morning. But I had no sooner opened my Bible and started to pray when exuberant voices, and loud *thump-thump-thumping* on the floor above me, forced me to put it aside.

"Be quiet! I'm trying to pray!"

I tried again.

I had just turned to Psalms and begun to read when the same sounds of war broke out.

"I told you once, and I'll tell you for the last time—be quiet! I'm trying to pray!"

Well, needless to say, I never got the chance to have devotions that morning.

Undeterred, I tried again the next morning. Bright and early, I tiptoed to the kitchen. Once again, no sooner had I started to read and pray than the boys came tearing into the kitchen, Christopher hot on Jason's heels. Jason was screaming, "Mom! Mom!"

"Can't you see I'm trying to have *quiet* time?"

Devotions—whether my own or the family's—were a huge challenge. I petitioned God, "Can't You keep them quiet long enough for me to have a quiet time?"

But that didn't work either.

I decided to storm the gates of heaven with a challenge: "If You can keep them quiet long enough for me to have a quiet time, I will be a better mother. You, Lord, know how important this is."

But it was not to be.

No time to pray! Prayers on the run became the norm. Not only did I need devotions more than ever during this time, but the fact that I wasn't doing them just piled on more guilt. My guilt caused more separation in my relationship with God, resulting in even more guilt. How could I free myself from this negative spiral?

I did some serious thinking and praying while folding the clothes. I asked myself, *Is it really true? Are daily devotions a required aspect of being a Christian? Or did Christ come to save us from the pressure to earn our salvation? Sure, the more time we spend in devotions, the easier it is to feel close to God. But are they essential? Are they a requirement?*

Perhaps I had been wrong in my assumption that I was not

a good Christian unless I had daily devotions. Had I, in fact, become an Old Testament Christian? Was accepting grace as a free gift too hard to do? As a result, did I begin to try to inadvertently earn my salvation by developing a list of rules to live by? Was it possible that God was allowing me to go through these trying times to learn to love my Lord and accept His salvation free of rules and regulations? Was God trying to free me from a restrictive faith?

After all, by trying to regulate my walk with God, by putting requirements into place that helped me feel I was contributing to my salvation, wasn't I negating the Cross? By feeling that I had to do my part, wasn't I in essence saying, "Your dying on the cross was not enough, Lord!"

Accepting His grace—without doing anything but accepting it—was the lesson I learned by not being able to do my devotions. Did my relationship with God suffer? I would say it was tested. It was forced to grow to a new dimension. I began to find, here and there, a Scripture that really spoke to me. I would scribble it on a piece of paper and post it on the refrigerator door. It usually stayed there for weeks, or even a month, until I found another verse to take its place. In the meantime, I could read it over and over again. The more I read it, the more it became a part of me.

My prayers those days were forged in the furnace of real life. My faith took on a new depth I would never have discovered without the daily challenges of being a Christian mother.

In ceramics, glazes reveal their true colors when they are subjected to the searing heat of a furnace. In much the same way, the true colors of my faith were revealed in the heat of putting it to work every day. My faith grew in spite of and, indeed, *because* I was forced to learn to pray on the run, internalize Scripture, and accept God's grace unconditionally.

~~~~~~

> *No time to read my Bible.*
> *No time to pray.*
> *God loves me — anyway!*

~~~~~~

Christ is the end of the law so that there may be righteousness
for everyone who believes.

—Romans 10:4

Lord,
Thank You for teaching me
So much about
      Your love
      Your grace
      Your majesty

Thank You for saving me
      Freely
      Without strings attached

Thank You for putting my faith
      Through trying times
      Through growing times
      Through firing times

So, I can become the woman You need me to be
A Christian mother—
Truly free from
      Self-imposed requirements
      Self-initiated regulations
      Self-adopted contributions

Attempts to feel worthy of my salvation
How foolish since
You have already paid the price
You have made the impossible possible
Through Your death
And resurrection

I love You, Lord.
I accept Your grace
Every day

Amen.

Just Say Yes — to the Gift of Grace!

*I*t was late at night. My husband and I had finished the dishes. There were just the two of us left at home now. Jim had asked me, as he did every night after work, "Have you heard from the boys today?"

I usually saw Jason every day. He was living at home (per our recommendation) so he could study for the bar without having to work. Chris usually called once a week from seminary to let me know if I needed to add anything to the grocery list for when he came home for the weekend. I make a point of calling Scott regularly since he had been sworn in as a police officer. My little blond cello player, who was never allowed to play with even water guns, now carries real guns and bullets. As a result, I find I need to hear his voice on a regular basis. And when my cell rings and I see Nick's name on the screen, that can mean only one thing. He needs more money put into his account for architectural supplies at USC.

It was after my sons were all out of the house that I entered a doctoral program. In the process I became conditioned to checking my e-mail every night before going to bed. I had formed friendships with the other doctoral students in the program as we encouraged one another through the grueling process. But I was unprepared for the e-mail that popped up in my in-box that evening. It was from a young father I had met in my doctoral program. The e-mail was titled simply "My Mother."

Kurt wrote, "Never in a million years did I think I would be writing you to ask this favor of you. My mother was diagnosed four months ago with stage-four brain cancer. She has maybe a few weeks to live. She does not have a home church, but she visited the Crystal Cathedral for Christmas and Easter. Would it be possible for us to have Mom's service at the cathedral? It would mean so much to her and to us."

I wiped the tears from my eyes and wrote back immediately. Of course I would help make those arrangements for him. I also told him I would be happy to bring a pastor from the church to visit and pray with her.

The next morning there was a voice mail on my cell. It was from Kurt's wife. "Sheila, it would mean so much to us if you could bring a pastor. Mom hasn't had anything to eat or drink in two days. It won't be much longer."

I called Bob Cavinder, a pastor at our church. It was his day off. "It's okay, Sheila. If you feel God is prodding us to go today, I will go with you."

Kurt opened the door to us. His eyes were red from crying, as were his brother's, his father's, and his wife's. Behind a screen in the living room lay his mother, Julia. The screen that shielded her bed was papered with an assortment of colorful get-well cards. It was obvious this was a woman who was well loved. Kurt and his brother told Bob and me stories of their mother, her love of the ocean and how much she loved her two boys. Kurt told us how she had taught them how to surf when they were little.

Even though her hair was gone, she still looked beautiful. There was not a wrinkle on her soft, transparent skin. Her cheeks were full and plump and even rosy. But her eyes were closed and she gave no indication she knew we were there looking down at her, studying her, talking about her. I said to Kurt, "Do you mind if I pray for your mom?"

His voice choked, a tear slid down his cheek. He could merely nod an assent.

I placed my hand on her soft bald head. I had expected the stubble to be prickly, but it felt like the fuzz of a newborn baby. A lump welled up in my throat. I swallowed hard, and with great effort began to recite the Twenty-third Psalm as my hand remained softly touching Julia's head:

> The LORD is my shepherd;
>> I shall not be in want.
> He makes me lie down in green pastures;
>> he leads me beside quiet waters,
> he restores my soul.
>> He guides me in paths of righteousness
>> for his name's sake.
> Even though I walk through
>> the valley of the shadow of death,
> I will fear no evil,
>> for you are with me;
> your rod and your staff,
>> they comfort me.
> You prepare a table before me
>> in the presence of my enemies.

You anoint my head with oil;
>   my cup overflows.
Surely goodness and love will follow me
>   all the days of my life,
and I will dwell in the house of the LORD forever.

"Lord God, cradle Your precious daughter Julia. Hold her in Your arms. Prepare her for her final homecoming. Comfort her sons and her husband, who grieve losing their beloved mother and wife. We love her, Lord. Thank You for her amazing life, her treasured sons. May they be comforted with the many wonderful memories they have of her. And may they be assured that her life is not ending, but just beginning anew in heaven with You. Amen."

I haltingly said the psalm and the prayer, my voice becoming more and more choked. My words were interspersed with sobs from grown men — her boys. When I turned to face them they were weeping openly, grieving over the imminent loss of their mother. I held Kurt in my arms.

Then I asked him, "Would you like Bob to baptize your mother?"

Wiping tears from a drenched face, he nodded. "Yes. We would like that very much."

Then Kurt leaned over his mother and said, "Mom, would you like to be baptized?"

Amazingly, Julia's startling blue eyes popped open with clarity. She looked right at him. With a surprisingly strong voice she said, "Yes."

Bob leaned over and asked her, "Julia, do you accept Jesus Christ as your Lord and Savior?"

"Yes."

"Do you repent of your sins and promise to live for Him?"

"Yes."

Dipping his fingers in the bowl of water (which Kurt's wife had hastily retrieved from the kitchen per our request), he made a transparent, glistening cross on her forehead. "I baptize you, Julia, in the name of the Father, the Son, and the Holy Spirit. Amen."

Even though we all were stunned by the beauty of what we had just witnessed, Bob turned to Kurt and the others in the room and asked if they would also like to be baptized. Kurt and his wife said, "Yes. We would love to be baptized."

Bob asked them, "Do you believe in Jesus Christ as your Lord and Savior?"

With tears running down their cheeks, they said yes.

"Do you repent and promise to live for Him?"

"Yes."

Dipping his fingers into the bowl, Bob etched a cross with water on each of their foreheads, saying, "I baptize you in the name of the Father, the Son, and the Holy Spirit."

John, the second son, had been quietly looking on. Bob asked, "Would you like to be baptized?"

He looked down and shuffled his feet nervously. "No, I'm okay."

We put the bowl down on the coffee table and rejoiced with them in their mother's baptism. John was quiet and tense as we continued to reassure them of their mother's salvation and the fact that she was now ready to make her final homecoming. It was when we turned to leave that John suddenly said, "Wait! Please, I would like to be baptized."

So Bob picked up the bowl. He smiled at John and asked

him, "Do you, John, believe in Jesus Christ as your Lord and Savior?"

Tears running in rivulets poured from his eyes. His lips trembled as he said, "Yes."

"Do you repent and promise to live for Him?"

"Yes."

"Then I baptize you, John, in the name of the Father, the Son, and the Holy Spirit. Amen."

Amazingly, throughout her baptism and the baptisms of her children, Julia watched intently from her deathbed. Unable to lift her head, she followed us with her eyes throughout the small room. But when Bob baptized John and said "Amen," Julia's eyes closed for the last time. We heard later that she lived only two more days.

Julia, literally on her deathbed, accepted Jesus Christ as her Lord and Savior and was baptized. She lived just long enough to see her boys also accept Jesus and be baptized. Julia, Kurt, Lisa, and John—all said yes to grace!

As Kurt walked us to the car he reached out to me—just a colleague from a doctoral program—and said, words choked with tears, "Thank you, Sheila, for bringing God to my home. I had been thinking this is the end. Now I see it is just the beginning."

Julia had loved the ocean. She was a surfer, a real-life "Gidget." She taught her sons the love of nature, the sun, and the surf. She taught her sons to love life and live it to its fullest. But in the end, her final gift was her best gift. While she gave them the gift of life as a young mother years before, it was by saying yes to God's grace on her deathbed that she gave them the gift of eternal life. As they watched, she led the way and gave them the courage to follow. She taught them how to beat death at death's door. In the end, as she took her final breaths, she accepted and passed on to her sons the greatest gift of all: the gift of grace—the gift of life eternal!

Say yes to God!
Say yes to grace!
And receive the gift of eternal life
This—is the greatest gift
You can give your children!

I am persuaded that neither death nor life,
nor angels nor principalities nor powers,
nor things present nor things to come,
nor height nor depth, nor any other created thing,
shall be able to separate us from the love of God
which is in Christ Jesus our Lord.

—Romans 8:38–39 NKJV

Lord, Jesus Christ,
Thank You for the gift of life
For the fruit of my womb
My precious children!

I say "Yes" to You!
I say "Yes" to grace!
I say "Yes" to accepting
And passing on this gift
To those I love more than life itself

Help me to learn the lessons
So that I can teach them
The lessons they need to learn the most

So when I take my last breath
When I close my eyes for the last time

I can teach them not only how to live
But also how to say that final good-bye

So that when they face their final homecoming
They will be covered in Your grace
Your mercy
Your love
For all eternity!

                       Amen, amen, and amen.